THE PERFECT

WEESTA

AIR FRYER TOASTER OVEN

COOKBOOK

1000-DAY AFFORDABLE, QUICK & EASY RECIPES FOR BOTH BEGINNERS AND ADVANCED USERS

ISMAEL HEATH

CONTENTS

INTRODUCTION **8**

How Does Air Frying Work? 8

Seeing the Benefits of the WEESTA Air Fryer Oven 8

Tricks on How to Use the Accessories of the WEESTA Air Fryer Oven 9

BREAKFAST **12**

Strawberry Pie 12

Salmon Burgers 12

Garlic Cheese Pull-apart Bread 13

Tuscan Toast 13

Christmas Eggnog Bread 14

English Scones 14

Strawberry Bread 15

Breakfast Bars 15

Granola With Sesame And Sunflower Seeds 16

Broccoli Cornbread 16

Turkey And Tuna Melt 17

Savory Breakfast Bread Pudding 17

Sun-dried Tomato Spread 18

Baked Eggs And Bacon 18

English Muffins 19

Popovers 19

Classic Cinnamon Rolls 20

Italian Strata 21

Western Frittata 22

LUNCH AND DINNER **23**

Inspirational Personal Pizza 23

Sage, Chicken + Mushroom Pasta Casserole 24

Kasha Loaf 24

Zucchini Casserole 25

Glazed Pork Tenderloin With Carrots Sheet Pan Supper 26

French Onion Soup 27

Oven-baked Barley 27

Favorite Baked Ziti 28

Tarragon Beef Ragout 29

Kashaburgers 29

Crab Chowder 30

Connecticut Garden Chowder 30

Very Quick Pizza 31

Meat Lovers Pan Pizza 31

Rosemary Lentils 32

Baked Parsleyed Cheese Grits 32

Pesto Pizza 33

Roasted Harissa Chicken + Vegetables 34

Chicken Noodle Soup 35

SNACKS APPETIZERS AND SIDES **36**

Classic Potato Chips 36

Asparagus With Pistachio Dukkah 37

Fried Apple Wedges 38

Skinny Fries 38

Baked Spicy Pimento Cheese Dip 39

Homemade Pretzel Bites 40

Sweet Apple Fries 41

Fried Green Tomatoes 42

Sweet Plantain Chips 43

Rosemary Roasted Vegetables 43

Breaded Zucchini 44

Foolproof Baked White Rice 44

Broiled Maryland Crabcakes With Creamy Herb Sauce 45

Creamy Parmesan Polenta 45

Mozzarella-stuffed Arancini 46

Sweet Chili– Glazed Wings 48

Cinnamon Pita Chips 48

Panko-breaded Onion Rings 49

Pork Belly Scallion Yakitori 50

FISH AND SEAFOOD **51**

    Bacon-wrapped Scallops 51

    Better Fish Sticks 51

    Mediterranean Baked Fish 52

    Miso-rubbed Salmon Fillets 52

    Crunchy Clam Strips 53

    Baked Parsley Mussels With Zucchini 53

    Tex-mex Fish Tacos 54

    Lobster Tails 54

    Tuna Nuggets In Hoisin Sauce 55

    Coconut Jerk Shrimp 56

    Crispy Calamari 57

    Almond-crusted Fish 58

    Sweet Chili Shrimp 58

    Fried Shrimp 59

    Marinated Catfish 59

    Shrimp With Jalapeño Dip 60

    Halibut Tacos 60

    Garlic-lemon Shrimp Skewers 61

    Crispy Sweet-and-sour Cod Fillets 61

POULTRY **62**

    Crispy Duck With Cherry Sauce 62

    Chicken In Mango Sauce 63

    Chicken Schnitzel Dogs 64

    Chicken Fajitas 65

    Air-fried Turkey Breast With Cherry Glaze 66

    Chicken Cutlets With Broccoli Rabe And Roasted Peppers 67

    Harissa Lemon Whole Chicken 68

    Chicken Wellington 69

    Roast Chicken 70

    Thai Chicken Drumsticks 71

    Foiled Rosemary Chicken Breasts 72

    Crispy Chicken Parmesan 72

    Chicken Breast With Chermoula Sauce 73

Sesame Chicken Breasts 74

Chicken Cordon Bleu 75

Buffalo Egg Rolls 76

Philly Chicken Cheesesteak Stromboli 77

Marinated Green Pepper And Pineapple Chicken 78

Peanut Butter-barbeque Chicken 79

BEEF PORK AND LAMB **80**

Smokehouse-style Beef Ribs 80

Traditional Pot Roast 80

Classic Pepperoni Pizza 81

Beef And Spinach Braciole 82

Stuffed Bell Peppers 83

Crispy Smoked Pork Chops 84

Ribeye Steak With Blue Cheese Compound Butter 85

Barbeque Ribs 85

Chipotle-glazed Meat Loaf 86

Albóndigas 87

Zesty London Broil 88

Pork Taco Gorditas 89

Lime-ginger Pork Tenderloin 90

Beef Al Carbon (street Taco Meat) 90

Pesto Pork Chops 91

Minted Lamb Chops 91

Pork Loin 92

Pretzel-coated Pork Tenderloin 92

Better-than-chinese-take-out Pork Ribs 93

VEGETABLES AND VEGETARIAN **94**

Parmesan Asparagus 94

Onions 94

Lentil-stuffed Zucchini 95

Broiled Tomatoes 96

Crisp Cajun Potato Wedges 96

Five-spice Roasted Sweet Potatoes 97

Mushrooms, Sautéed 97

Yellow Squash 98

Glazed Carrots 99

Ratatouille 99

Blistered Tomatoes 100

Tasty Golden Potatoes 100

Brown Rice And Goat Cheese Croquettes 101

Buttery Rolls 102

Roasted Vegetables 103

Marjoram New Potatoes 103

Mashed Potato Tots 104

Vegetable–goat Cheese Flatbreads 105

Fried Green Tomatoes With Sriracha Mayo 106

DESSERTS **107**

Cowboy Cookies 107

Chewy Brownies 108

Currant Carrot Cake 109

Blueberry Clafoutis 109

Giant Oatmeal–peanut Butter Cookie 110

Almond-roasted Pears 111

Orange Glaze 111

Lime Cheesecake 112

Easy Peach Turnovers 113

Keto Cheesecake Cups 114

Hasselback Apple Crisp 115

Individual Peach Crisps 116

Green Grape Meringues 116

Spice Cake 117

Gingerbread 118

Pineapple Tartlets 119

Blueberry Cookies 119

INTRODUCTION

How Does Air Frying Work?

Ever wonder why fried mozzarella sticks and potato chips get crunchy? All that hot oil causes the surface water in food to boil super-quick and exit as steam — leaving the outside of your food dry, which is the perfect setup for golden brown, crispy results.

Air fryers are full of hot air, literally. Air replaces oil in this machine and crisps and browns while it circulates around food. Air fried foods generally have less fat and calories per serving compared to their doppelganger fried version.

Seeing the Benefits of the WEESTA Air Fryer Oven

1. Protect the food's nutrients

Unlike deep frying, Air Fryers do not deconstruct the food's good nutrients and add on bad fats. If you think your yasai tempura (deep-fried battered vegetables) are healthy, here is news for you; while they may look like they are full of nutritious elements, the deep frying process would have destroyed the beneficial vitamins and minerals contained in the vegetables.

2. Keeping cancer at bay

For some oils (e.g. olive and flax seed), their chemical structure changes in high heat causing them to transform into bad forms of fat. Additionally, since there is little oil used, there is little chance for food to produce carcinogens that activate cancer cells.

3. Calories are good, but too much spells trouble!

Fried foods are high in calories which is the leading cause of weight gain and obesity. Obesity will then lead to a plethora of killer diseases such as diabetes, cancer, stroke, sleep problems, and immobility to name a few. Adopting a low-fat diet will help you maintain your weight or prevent weight loss because essentially, you are eating fewer calories. Therefore, eating Air Fryer-cooked food will support your weight loss journey.

4. Build a fortress for your heart

Eating food fried with an Air Fryer reduces the risk of heart diseases and protects your body by helping you absorb the necessary nutrients. Since a minimal amount of oil is used to prepare food, you can be sure that your body will not accumulate excessive fats in the long run. Instead, the optimal amount of oil used will help your body protect your heart.

5. Keeping your kidneys clear

Consuming excess amounts of deep-fried food will impair your kidney's ability to filter our harmful fats. Therefore, eating food fried by an Air Fryer can help you lower your risks of getting kidney disease. If you are finding it difficult to quit deep-fried food cold turkey, using an Air Fryer will ease your transition to a healthier diet.

6. Reduce the worries of fat

Fat is a macro nutrient – it is essential to help control inflammation, blood clotting, maintaining healthy hair and skin, prevent heart diseases, provide energy and assist in the absorption of vitamins A, D, E, and K. While it is important to your bodily functions, too much of it is detrimental to health. An Air Fryer is a modern kitchen appliance that fries food using heated hot air by using at most a tablespoon of oil. This way, you are able to eat fried food without worrying about the negative effects of fatty food on your health.

Tricks on How to Use the Accessories of the WEESTA Air Fryer Oven

1. Heating Element Protection Cover

The protection cover can prevent the food from contacting the heating element.

Let the side with wire handle face down, slide along the top plastic shelf near the heating element in the oven to install the protection cover. Take out the protection cover by pulling the wire handle.

2. Air Flow Racks

The air flow racks can be used not only for dehydration but also to cook crispy snacks or reheat foods like pizza.

Slide along the rack shelf to install or take out the air flow racks.

3. Rotisserie Fork Set

The rotisserie fork set is used for roasting large meat or whole chicken.

Install a fork backwards to the gear on the shaft. Force shaft lengthwise through meat/chicken in center. Install another fork towards the meat/chicken. Slide both forks into meat/chicken and adjust the meat/chicken to the middle of the shaft, then drive the screws to lock the forks in position.

You can adjust the forks closer to the middle if needed but never outwards to the groove of both ends.

To install the rotisserie fork set, let the end with the gear face towards left, insert the grooves on both ends of the shaft into the rotating shelf.

4. Rotisserie Basket

Great for fries, roasting nuts and other snacks.

Use the hasp to open and lock the rotisserie basket. To install the rotisserie basket, let the the gear face towards left, insert the grooves on both ends of the shaft into the rotating shelf.

5. Fetch Tool

Used to remove the rotisserie basket or fork set from the appliance.

Place the fetch tool under the shaft at both side of the rotisserie basket or fork set，then gently extract the rotisserie basket or fork set out.

6. Drip Tray

Cook with the drip tray for easy clean ups.

Put the drip tray into the bottom of the appliance when in use. It is easy to take out for cleaning.

7. Door

The door is detachable for easy cleaning.

Open the door at a 30°angle from the appliance and gently put on or take off the door.

The appliance will not work with the door open

- To keep your air fryer oven in good working order, make sure to remove all food residues and grease splatters from interior surfaces on a regular basis. Regular cleaning will also reduce the fire hazard risk.

➢ Unplug the air fryer oven from the power supply. Allow the appliance to cool.

➢ Remove all accessories (crumb tray, oven rack, food tray, air-frying basket, pizza pan) from the oven cavity.

Interior walls and oven door

➢ Use a damp cloth and mild detergent solution on a sponge to clean the interior walls and door of the air fryer oven. Repeat with a dry, clean cloth.

➢ Never use harsh abrasives, corrosive products or as these could damage the oven surface. Never use steel wool pads or other abrasive cleaning products. Abrasive cleaners, scrubbing brushes and chemical cleaners will damage the coating on this unit. Pieces can break off the and touch electrical parts involving a risk of electrical shock.

➢ If scrubbing is necessary, use a nonabrasive nylon or polyester mesh pad.

Crumb tray

➢ To remove crumbs and drippings from the bottom of the oven, slide out the crumb tray and discard any crumbs. Wipe the crumb tray clean and replace. To remove baked-on grease, soak the tray in hot, sudsy water or use nonabrasive cleaners. Never operate the oven without the crumb tray in place!

Exterior surfaces

➢ Wipe the appliance housing clean with a damp cloth and a mild detergent. Apply the cleansing agent to the cloth, not directly onto the oven. Dry thoroughly

BREAKFAST

Strawberry Pie

Servings: 6
Cooking Time: 25 Minutes

Ingredients:

- 2 16-ounce packages frozen sliced strawberries or 1 quart fresh strawberries, washed, stemmed, and sliced
- ¼ cup sugar
- 2 tablespoons lemon juice
- 2 tablespoons cornstarch
- 1 single Oatmeal Piecrust, baked (recipe follows)
- Strawberry Pie Glaze (recipe follows)

Directions:

1. Preheat the toaster oven to 350° F.
2. Combine the strawberries, sugar, lemon juice, and cornstarch in a medium bowl, mixing well. Fill the piecrust shell with the strawberries, spreading evenly.
3. BAKE for 25 minutes, or until the strawberries are tender. Glaze with Strawberry Pie Glaze.

Salmon Burgers

Servings: 4
Cooking Time: 25 Minutes

Ingredients:

- ¾ cup Homemade Bread Crumbs
- 1 15-ounce can salmon, drained
- 1 small zucchini, finely chopped
- 2 tablespoons finely chopped onions
- 1 egg
- 1 teaspoon dried rosemary
- 1 teaspoon lemon juice
- 1 teaspoon garlic powder
- Salt and freshly ground black pepper to taste
- 1 teaspoon vegetable oil

Directions:

1. Preheat the toaster oven to 400° F.
2. Blend all ingredients except the oil and form patties 1½ inches thick. Place on an oiled or nonstick 8½ × 8½ × 2-inch square baking (cake) pan.
3. BAKE for 25 minutes, or until the patties are lightly browned.

Garlic Cheese Pull-apart Bread

Servings: 6
Cooking Time: 26 Minutes

Ingredients:

- 1 (1-pound) loaf frozen white bread dough
- Canola or vegetable oil
- Nonstick cooking spray
- 6 tablespoons unsalted butter, melted
- 3 cloves garlic, finely minced
- 2 tablespoons minced fresh flat-leaf (Italian) parsley
- ¼ teaspoon table salt
- ¼ teaspoon freshly ground black pepper
- ⅔ cup shredded Parmesan cheese
- ¾ cup shredded mozzarella cheese

Directions:

1. Rub the frozen dough lightly with the oil. Place it in a zip-top bag and refrigerate overnight to thaw.
2. Spray a 9 x 5-inch loaf pan with nonstick cooking spray.
3. Stir the butter, garlic, parsley, salt, and pepper in a small bowl; set aside.
4. Place the thawed dough on a lightly floured board and roll into a 12-inch square. Brush about 3 tablespoons of the butter mixture over the top of the dough. Sprinkle evenly with about ½ cup Parmesan and ½ cup mozzarella. Roll the dough over the filling, jelly-roll style. Cut into rolls ½ to ¾ inch thick. Stand the rolls upright in the loaf pan, two across, with the cut side of the rolls facing the narrow end of the pan. (There will be two rows, side by side, with 8 to 10 rolls in each row.) Cover with a towel and let rise for about 1 hour.
5. Preheat the toaster oven to 350°F. Bake for 18 to 23 minutes, or until the loaf is golden brown. Drizzle with the remaining melted butter mixture. Sprinkle with the remaining 2 tablespoons Parmesan cheese and the remaining¼ cup mozzarella cheese. Bake for 2 to 3 minutes for the cheese to melt.
6. Place the pan on a wire rack and let stand for 5 minutes. Remove the loaf from the pan. Serve warm.

Tuscan Toast

Servings: 4
Cooking Time: 5 Minutes

Ingredients:

- ¼ cup butter
- ½ teaspoon lemon juice
- ½ clove garlic
- ½ teaspoon dried parsley flakes
- 4 slices Italian bread, 1-inch thick

Directions:

1. Place butter, lemon juice, garlic, and parsley in a food processor. Process about 1 minute, or until garlic is pulverized and ingredients are well blended.
2. Spread garlic butter on both sides of bread slices.
3. Place bread slices upright in air fryer oven. (They can lie flat but cook better standing on end.)
4. Air-fry at 390°F for 5minutes or until toasty brown.

Christmas Eggnog Bread

Servings: 6

Cooking Time: 18 Minutes

Ingredients:

- 1 cup flour, plus more for dusting
- ¼ cup sugar
- 1 teaspoon baking powder
- ¼ teaspoon salt
- ¼ teaspoon nutmeg
- ½ cup eggnog
- 1 egg yolk
- 1 tablespoon butter, plus 1 teaspoon, melted
- ¼ cup pecans
- ¼ cup chopped candied fruit (cherries, pineapple, or mixed fruits)
- cooking spray

Directions:

1. Preheat the toaster oven to 360°F.
2. In a medium bowl, stir together the flour, sugar, baking powder, salt, and nutmeg.
3. Add eggnog, egg yolk, and butter. Mix well but do not beat.
4. Stir in nuts and fruit.
5. Spray a 6 x 6-inch baking pan with cooking spray and dust with flour.
6. Spread batter into prepared pan and air-fry at 360°F for 18 minutes or until top is dark golden brown and bread starts to pull away from sides of pan.

English Scones

Servings: 8

Cooking Time: 8 Minutes

Ingredients:

- 2 cups all-purpose flour
- 1 tablespoon baking powder
- ½ teaspoon salt
- 2 tablespoons sugar
- ¼ cup unsalted butter
- ⅔ cup plus 1 tablespoon whole milk, divided

Directions:

1. Preheat the toaster oven to 380°F.
2. In a large bowl, whisk together the flour, baking powder, salt, and sugar. Using a pastry blender or your fingers, cut in the butter until pea-size crumbles appear. Make a well in the center and pour in ⅔ cup of the milk. Quickly mix the batter until a ball forms. Knead the dough 3 times.
3. Place the dough onto a floured surface and, using your hands or a rolling pin, flatten the dough until it's ¾ inch thick. Using a biscuit cutter or drinking glass, cut out 10 circles, reforming the dough and flattening as needed to use up the batter.
4. Brush the tops lightly with the remaining 1 tablespoon of milk.
5. Place the scones into the air fryer oven. Air-fry for 8 minutes or until golden brown and cooked in the center.

Strawberry Bread

Servings: 6

Cooking Time: 28 Minutes

Ingredients:

- ½ cup frozen strawberries in juice, completely thawed (do not drain)
- 1 cup flour
- ½ cup sugar
- 1 teaspoon cinnamon
- ½ teaspoon baking soda
- ⅛ teaspoon salt
- 1 egg, beaten
- ⅓ cup oil
- cooking spray

Directions:

1. Cut any large berries into smaller pieces no larger than ½ inch.
2. Preheat the toaster oven to 330°F.
3. In a large bowl, stir together the flour, sugar, cinnamon, soda, and salt.
4. In a small bowl, mix together the egg, oil, and strawberries. Add to dry ingredients and stir together gently.
5. Spray 6 x 6-inch baking pan with cooking spray.
6. Pour batter into prepared pan and air-fry at 330°F for 28 minutes.
7. When bread is done, let cool for 10 minutes before removing from pan.

Breakfast Bars

Servings: 6

Cooking Time: 35 Minutes

Ingredients:

- 1 cup unsweetened applesauce
- 1 carrot, peeled and grated
- ½ cup raisins
- 1 egg
- 1 tablespoon vegetable oil
- 2 tablespoons molasses
- 2 tablespoons brown sugar
- ¼ cup chopped walnuts
- 2 cups rolled oats
- 2 tablespoons sesame seeds
- 1 teaspoon ground cinnamon
- ¼ teaspoon grated nutmeg
- ¼ teaspoon ground ginger
- Salt to taste

Directions:

1. Preheat the toaster oven to 375° F.
2. Combine all the ingredients in a bowl, stirring well to blend. Press the mixture into an oiled or nonstick 8½ × 8½ × 2inch square baking (cake) pan.
3. BAKE for 35 minutes, or until golden brown. Cool and cut into squares.

Granola With Sesame And Sunflower Seeds

Servings: 4
Cooking Time: 20 Minutes

Ingredients:

- 2 cups rolled oats
- ½ cup sunflower seeds
- ½ cup sesame seeds
- ½ cup unsweetened shredded
- Coconut
- ½ cup slivered almonds
- ½ cup honey
- 1 tablespoon vegetable oil
- 1 teaspoon toasted sesame oil
- 1 teaspoon ground cinnamon
- Pinch of grated nutmeg
- Salt to taste

Directions:

1. Preheat the toaster oven to 375° F.
2. Combine all the granola ingredients in a large bowl, mixing well.
3. Spread the mixture evenly in an oiled or nonstick 6½ × 6½ × 2-inch square (cake) pan.
4. BAKE for 20 minutes, turning the ingredients every 5 minutes with tongs to toast evenly. Cool and store in an airtight container in the refrigerator.

Broccoli Cornbread

Servings: 6
Cooking Time: 18 Minutes

Ingredients:

- 1 cup frozen chopped broccoli, thawed and drained
- ¼ cup cottage cheese
- 1 egg, beaten
- 2 tablespoons minced onion
- 2 tablespoons melted butter
- ½ cup flour
- ½ cup yellow cornmeal
- 1 teaspoon baking powder
- ½ teaspoon salt
- ¼ cup milk, plus 2 tablespoons
- cooking spray

Directions:

1. Place thawed broccoli in colander and press with a spoon to squeeze out excess moisture.
2. Stir together all ingredients in a large bowl.
3. Spray 6 x 6-inch baking pan with cooking spray.
4. Spread batter in pan and air-fry at 330°F for 18 minutes or until cornbread is lightly browned and loaf starts to pull away from sides of pan.

Turkey And Tuna Melt

Servings: 2

Cooking Time: 4 Minutes

Ingredients:

- 4 slices multigrain bread Spicy brown mustard
- 1 6-ounce can tuna in water, drained well and crumbled
- ¼ pound thinly sliced turkey breast
- 4 slices low-fat Monterey Jack cheese
- 2 tablespoons finely chopped scallions
- Salt and freshly ground black pepper

Directions:

1. Spread one side of each bread slice with mustard and place on an oiled or nonstick
2. 6½ × 10-inch baking sheet.
3. Layer 2 slices with equal portions of tuna, turkey, cheese, and scallion. Season to taste with salt and pepper.
4. TOAST twice, or until the cheese is melted.

Savory Breakfast Bread Pudding

Servings: 4

Cooking Time: 30 Minutes

Ingredients:

- Oil spray (hand-pumped)
- 4 slices whole-wheat bread, cubed
- 1 cup frozen potato hash browns, thawed
- 5 large eggs
- 1 cup whole milk
- ½ cup diced ham
- ½ cup shredded cheddar cheese
- 1 teaspoon fresh parsley, chopped
- ⅛ teaspoon sea salt
- ⅛ teaspoon freshly ground black pepper

Directions:

1. Place the baking tray on position 1 and preheat the toaster oven on BAKE to 350°F for 5 minutes.
2. Lightly oil an 8-inch-square baking dish with spray.
3. Spread the bread cubes and potatoes in the baking dish evenly.
4. In a medium bowl, combine the eggs, milk, ham, cheese, parsley, salt, and pepper.
5. Pour the egg mixture over the bread and potatoes in the dish.
6. Bake for 30 minutes. The bread pudding should be lightly golden, the eggs set, and a knife inserted in the center should come out clean.
7. Cool the pudding for 5 minutes and serve.

Sun-dried Tomato Spread

Servings: 1

Cooking Time: 4 Minutes

Ingredients:

- ½ cup minced sun-dried tomatoes
- 3 tablespoons olive oil
- 2 tablespoons grated Parmesan cheese
- 1 teaspoon dried oregano or
- 1 tablespoon chopped fresh oregano
- 3 tablespoons chopped pecans or walnuts
- 2 garlic cloves, chopped
- Salt and freshly ground black pepper to taste

Directions:

1. Combine the sun-dried tomatoes and ⅔ cup water in an oiled or nonstick 8½ × 8½ × 2-inch baking (cake) pan.

2. BROIL for 4 minutes, or until the tomatoes are softened. Remove from the oven and transfer the tomatoes with the liquid to a bowl. Add all the other ingredients and mix well.

3. Process the mixture in a blender or food processor until smooth. Adjust the seasonings.

Baked Eggs And Bacon

Servings: 2

Cooking Time: 25 Minutes

Ingredients:

- 8 slices bacon
- 4 large eggs
- 2 teaspoons fresh chives or scallion greens, chopped
- Sea salt, for seasoning
- Freshly ground black pepper, for seasoning

Directions:

1. Place the baking tray on position 1 and preheat the toaster oven on BAKE to 400°F for 5 minutes.

2. Arrange the bacon slices in four (4-ounce) ramekins, 2 per cup. Overlap the slices over the bottom and sides so that as much of the cup is covered as possible.

3. Bake for 10 to 15 minutes. The fat will start to render, and the bacon will start to crisp and brown on the edges. Take the ramekins out of the oven and lightly blot any excess oil in the bottom of each one.

4. Crack 1 egg into each cup, sprinkle with chives, and season lightly with salt and pepper.

5. Bake for 10 minutes, or until the egg yolks reach the desired consistency.

6. Take them out of the oven and run a knife around the edge of each cup to loosen and remove from the ramekin. Serve.

English Muffins

Servings: 2

Cooking Time: 4 Minutes

Ingredients:

- 1 English muffin, split
- 1 plum tomato, chopped
- 2 slices reduced-fat or low-fat cheese
- 2 slices reduced-fat honey ham
- 1 tablespoon chopped fresh parsley

Directions:

1. Layer each muffin half with equal portions of tomato, cheese, and ham. Place on a broiling rack with a pan underneath.
2. TOAST once.
3. Garnish each with equal portions of chopped parsley.

Popovers

Servings: 6

Cooking Time: 30 Minutes

Ingredients:

- 2 eggs
- 1 cup skim milk
- 2 tablespoons vegetable oil
- 1 cup unbleached flour
- Salt to taste

Directions:

1. Preheat the toaster oven to 400° F.
2. Beat all the ingredients in a medium bowl with an electric mixer at high speed until smooth. The batter should be the consistency of heavy cream.
3. Fill the pans of a 6-muffin tin three-quarters full.
4. BAKE for 20 minutes, then reduce the heat to 350° F. and bake for 10 minutes, or until golden brown.

Classic Cinnamon Rolls

Servings: 4

Cooking Time: 6 Minutes

Ingredients:

- 1½ cups all-purpose flour
- 1 tablespoon granulated sugar
- 2 teaspoons baking powder
- ½ teaspoon salt
- 4 tablespoons butter, divided
- ½ cup buttermilk
- 2 tablespoons brown sugar
- 1 teaspoon cinnamon
- 1 cup powdered sugar
- 2 tablespoons milk

Directions:

1. Preheat the toaster oven to 360°F.
2. In a large bowl, stir together the flour, sugar, baking powder, and salt. Cut in 3 tablespoons of the butter with a pastry blender or two knives until coarse crumbs remain. Stir in the buttermilk until a dough forms.
3. Place the dough onto a floured surface and roll out into a square shape about ½ inch thick.
4. Melt the remaining 1 tablespoon of butter in the microwave for 20 seconds. Using a pastry brush or your fingers, spread the melted butter onto the dough.
5. In a small bowl, mix together the brown sugar and cinnamon. Sprinkle the mixture across the surface of the dough. Roll the dough up, forming a long log. Using a pastry cutter or sharp knife, cut 10 cinnamon rolls.
6. Carefully place the cinnamon rolls into the air fryer oven. Then bake at 360°F for 6 minutes or until golden brown.
7. Meanwhile, in a small bowl, whisk together the powdered sugar and milk.
8. Plate the cinnamon rolls and drizzle the glaze over the surface before serving.

Italian Strata

Servings: 6

Cooking Time: 55 Minutes

Ingredients:

- 1 cup boiling water
- 3 tablespoons chopped sun-dried tomatoes (dry-packed)
- 5 cups cubed French bread or country bread (cut into 1-inch cubes)
- Nonstick cooking spray
- 1 ½ ounces sliced turkey pepperoni, cut into fourths (about ¾ cup)
- 2 tablespoons chopped pepperoncini peppers
- 1 cup coarsely chopped fresh spinach
- 1 cup shredded Italian blend cheese or mozzarella cheese
- 4 large eggs
- 1 ½ cups whole milk
- 1 teaspoon Italian seasoning
- ¼ teaspoon kosher salt
- 2 tablespoons shredded Parmesan cheese

Directions:

1. Pour the boiling water the over sun-dried tomatoes in a small, deep bowl; set aside.

2. Preheat the toaster oven to 350 °F. Place the bread cubes on a 12 x 12-inch baking pan. Bake for 10 minutes, stirring once.

3. Spray an 8 x 8-inch square baking pan with nonstick cooking spray. Drain the sun-dried tomatoes and pat dry with paper towels. Arrange half the bread cubes evenly in the prepared pan. Top with half the pepperoni, half the pepperoncini, all the spinach, and all of the reconstituted tomatoes. Sprinkle with ½ cup of the Italian cheese. Repeat layers with the remaining bread, pepperoni, pepperoncini, and ½ cup cheese.

4. Whisk the eggs, milk, Italian seasoning, and salt in a large bowl. Pour the egg mixture over the bread layers. Press down lightly with the back of a large spoon. Sprinkle with the Parmesan cheese. Cover and chill for at least 2 hours or overnight.

5. Preheat the toaster oven to 350°F. Bake the strata, uncovered, for 35 to 45 minutes, or until a knife inserted into the center comes out clean. Let stand for 10 minutes before serving.

Western Frittata

Servings: 1
Cooking Time: 19 Minutes

Ingredients:

- ½ red or green bell pepper, cut into ½-inch chunks
- 1 teaspoon olive oil
- 3 eggs, beaten
- ¼ cup grated Cheddar cheese
- ¼ cup diced cooked ham
- salt and freshly ground black pepper, to taste
- 1 teaspoon butter
- 1 teaspoon chopped fresh parsley

Directions:

1. Preheat the toaster oven to 400°F.

2. Toss the peppers with the olive oil and air-fry for 6 minutes, redistribute the ingredients once or twice during the process.

3. While the vegetables are cooking, beat the eggs well in a bowl, stir in the Cheddar cheese and ham, and season with salt and freshly ground black pepper. Add the air-fried peppers to this bowl when they have finished cooking.

4. Place a 6- or 7-inch non-stick metal cake pan into the air fryer oven with the butter using an aluminum sling to lower the pan into the air fryer oven. (Fold a piece of aluminum foil into a strip about 2-inches wide by 24-inches long.) Air-fry for 1 minute at 380°F to melt the butter. Remove the cake pan and rotate the pan to distribute the butter and grease the pan. Pour the egg mixture into the cake pan and return the pan to the air fryer oven, using the aluminum sling.

5. Air-fry at 380°F for 12 minutes, or until the frittata has puffed up and is lightly browned. Let the frittata sit in the air fryer oven for 5 minutes to cool to an edible temperature and set up. Remove the cake pan from the air fryer oven, sprinkle with parsley and serve immediately.

LUNCH AND DINNER

Inspirational Personal Pizza

Servings: 1
Cooking Time: 30 Minutes

Ingredients:
- 1 9-inch ready-made pizza crust
- 1 teaspoon olive oil
- 2 tablespoons tomato paste
- 4 ounces (½ cup) ground lean turkey breast
- 2 tablespoons sliced marinated artichokes
- 2 tablespoons pitted and chopped kalamata olives
- 2 tablespoons crumbled feta cheese
- 1 tablespoon chopped fresh basil leaves
- 1 tablespoon chopped fresh oregano leaves
- 2 tablespoons grated Parmesan cheese
- ¼ teaspoon red pepper flakes

Directions:
1. Preheat the toaster oven to 375°F.
2. Brush the pizza crust with the olive oil and spread on the tomato paste. Add all the other ingredients. Place the pizza on the toaster oven rack.
3. BAKE for 30 minutes, or until the topping is cooked and the crust is lightly browned.

Sage, Chicken + Mushroom Pasta Casserole

Servings: 6
Cooking Time: 35 Minutes

Ingredients:

- Nonstick cooking spray
- 8 ounces bow-tie pasta, uncooked
- 4 tablespoons unsalted butter
- 8 ounces button or white mushrooms, sliced
- 3 tablespoons all-purpose flour
- Kosher salt and freshly ground black pepper
- 2 cups whole milk
- ½ cup dry white wine
- 2 tablespoons minced fresh sage
- 1 ½ cups chopped cooked chicken
- 1 cup shredded fontina, Monterey Jack, or Swiss cheese
- ½ cup shredded Parmesan cheese

Directions:

1. Preheat the toaster oven to 350°F. Spray a 2-quart baking pan with nonstick cooking spray.

2. Cook the pasta according to the package directions; drain and set aside.

3. Melt the butter in a large skillet over medium-high heat. Add the mushrooms and cook, stirring frequently, until the liquid has evaporated, 7 to 10 minutes. Blend in the flour and cook, stirring constantly, for 1 minute. Season with salt and pepper. Gradually stir in the milk and wine. Cook, stirring constantly, until the mixture bubbles and begins to thicken. Remove from the heat. Stir in the sage, cooked pasta, chicken, and fontina. Season with salt and pepper.

4. Spoon into the prepared pan. Cover and bake for 25 to 30 minutes. Uncover, sprinkle with the Parmesan, and bake for an additional 5 minutes or until the cheese is melted.

5. Remove from the oven and let stand for 5 to 10 minutes before serving.

Kasha Loaf

Servings: 4
Cooking Time: 30 Minutes

Ingredients:

- 1 cup whole grain kasha
- 2 cups tomato sauce or 3 2 8-ounce cans tomato sauce (add a small amount of water to make 4 2 cups)
- 3 tablespoons minced onion or scallions
- 1 tablespoon minced garlic
- 1 cup multigrain bread crumbs
- 1 egg
- 1 teaspoon paprika
- 1 teaspoon chili powder
- 1 teaspoon sesame oil

Directions:

1. Preheat the toaster oven to 400° F.

2. Combine all the ingredients in a bowl and transfer to an oiled or nonstick regular-size 4½ × 8½ × 2/4-inch loaf pan.

3. BAKE, uncovered, for 30 minutes, or until lightly browned.

Zucchini Casserole

Servings: 4

Cooking Time: 37 Minutes

Ingredients:

- 4 small zucchini squashes, halved and quartered
- 2 plum tomatoes, quartered
- 1 8-ounce can tomato sauce
- 2 tablespoons chopped onion
- 2 garlic cloves, minced
- 1 tablespoon olive oil
- 1 tablespoon chopped fresh oregano
- 1 tablespoon chopped fresh basil
- 2 tablespoons pine nuts (pignoli)
- Salt and freshly ground black pepper to taste
- ½ cup shredded low-fat mozzarella cheese

Directions:

1. Preheat the toaster oven to 400° F.

2. Combine all the ingredients, except the mozzarella cheese, in a 1-quart 8½ × 8½ × 4-inch ovenproof baking dish. Cover with aluminum foil.

3. BAKE, covered, for 30 minutes, or until the zucchini is tender. Uncover and sprinkle the top with the cheese.

4. BROIL for 7 minutes, or until the cheese is melted and lightly browned.

Glazed Pork Tenderloin With Carrots Sheet Pan Supper

Servings: 4-6

Cooking Time: 20 Minutes

Ingredients:

- 1 pound pork tenderloin
- 1 teaspoon steak seasoning blend
- 2 large carrots, sliced 1/2-inch thick
- 2 large parsnips, sliced 1/2-inch thick
- 1/2 small sweet onion, cut in thin wedges
- 1 tablespoon olive oil
- Salt and pepper to taste
- 1/2 cup apricot jam
- 1 tablespoon balsamic vinegar

Directions:

1. Place rack on bottom position of toaster oven. Heat the toaster oven to 425°F. Spray the toaster oven baking pan with nonstick cooking spray or line the pan with nonstick aluminum foil.

2. Place pork tenderloin diagonally in center of pan. Sprinkle pork with seasoning blend.

3. In a large bowl, combine carrots, parsnips and onion. Add olive oil, salt and black pepper and stir until vegetables are coated. Arrange vegetables evenly in pan around pork.

4. Bake 20 minutes. Stir vegetables.

5. Meanwhile, in a small bowl, combine apricot jam and balsamic vinegar. Spoon about half of mixture over pork.

6. Continue baking until pork reaches reaches 160°F when tested with a meat thermometer and vegetables are roasted, about 10 minutes. Slice pork and serve with remaining sauce, if desired.

French Onion Soup

Servings: 4

Cooking Time: 46 Minutes

Ingredients:

- 1 cup finely chopped onions
- 1 teaspoon toasted sesame oil
- 1 tablespoon vegetable oil
- 2 ½ cup dry white wine
- 3 teaspoons soy sauce
- ½ teaspoon garlic powder
- Freshly ground black pepper to taste
- 4 French bread rounds, sliced 1 inch thick
- 4 tablespoons grated Parmesan cheese
- 1 tablespoon chopped fresh parsley

Directions:

1. Place the onions, sesame oil, and vegetable oil in an 8½ × 8½ × 2-inch square baking (cake) pan.

2. BROIL for 10 minutes, stirring every 3 minutes until the onions are tender. Remove from the oven and transfer to a 1-quart 8½ × 8½ × 4-inch ovenproof baking dish. Add 2 cups water, the wine, and the soy sauce. Add the garlic powder and pepper and adjust the seasonings.

3. BAKE, covered, at 400° F. for 30 minutes. Remove from the oven, uncover, and add the 4 bread rounds, letting them float on top of the soup. Sprinkle each with 1 tablespoon Parmesan cheese.

4. BROIL, uncovered, for 6 minutes, or until the cheese is lightly browned. With tongs, transfer the bread rounds to 4 individual soup bowls. Ladle the soup on top of the bread rounds. Garnish with the parsley and serve immediately.

Oven-baked Barley

Servings: 2

Cooking Time: 60 Minutes

Ingredients:

- ⅓ cup barley, toasted
- Seasonings:
- 1 tablespoon sesame oil
- 1 tablespoon sesame seeds
- ¼ teaspoon ground cumin
- ¼ teaspoon turmeric
- ½ teaspoon garlic powder
- Salt and freshly ground black pepper to taste

Directions:

1. Combine the barley and 1½ cups water in a 1-quart 8½ × 8½ × 4-inch ovenproof baking dish. Cover with aluminum foil.

2. BAKE, covered, for 50 minutes, or until almost cooked, testing the grains after 30 minutes for softness.

3. Add the oil and seasonings and fluff with a fork to combine. Cover and let the barley sit for 10 minutes to finish cooking and absorb the flavors of the seasonings. Fluff once more before serving.

Favorite Baked Ziti

Servings: 4

Cooking Time: 30 Minutes

Ingredients:
- 2 tablespoons olive oil
- 1 small onion, diced
- 3 cloves garlic, minced
- ¼ teaspoon red pepper flakes
- 1 pound lean ground beef
- ½ teaspoon kosher salt
- ¼ cup dry red wine
- 1 (14.5-ounce) can crushed tomatoes
- 1 tablespoon tomato paste
- 16 ounces ziti, uncooked
- Nonstick cooking spray
- ⅓ cup grated Parmesan cheese
- 1 ½ cups shredded mozzarella cheese
- 2 ounces fresh mozzarella cheese, cut into cubes (about ½ cup)

Directions:
1. Heat the olive oil in a large skillet over medium-high heat. Add the onion and cook, stirring frequently, until tender, 3 to 4 minutes. Stir in the garlic and red pepper flakes. Add the ground beef and salt. Cook, breaking up the ground beef, until the meat is brown and cooked through. Drain well, if needed, and return to the skillet.
2. Add the wine and cook for 2 minutes. Add the tomatoes, tomato paste, and ¾ cup water. Reduce the heat and simmer, uncovered, for 20 to 25 minutes, stirring occasionally.
3. Cook the ziti according to the package directions, except reduce the cooking time to 7 minutes. The ziti will be harder than Al Dente, which is what you want. Drain and rinse under cold water. Transfer to a large bowl.
4. Preheat the toaster oven to 425 ºF. Spray an 11 x 7 x 2 ½-inch baking dish with nonstick cooking spray. Spoon about 1 cup of the meat sauce into the prepared dish. Add half of the ziti in an even layer. Spoon about half of the remaining sauce over the ziti. Sprinkle with half the Parmesan and all the shredded mozzarella. Add the remaining half of ziti and cover with the remaining sauce. Sprinkle the remaining Parmesan on top.
5. Bake, covered, for 20 minutes. Remove from the oven and add the cubes of fresh mozzarella. Bake, uncovered, for an additional 10 minutes. If desired, turn to broil for a few minutes to make the top crispy and brown.
6. Remove from the oven and let stand for 10 minutes before serving.

Tarragon Beef Ragout

Servings: 6

Cooking Time: 53 Minutes

Ingredients:

- 1 pound lean round steak, cut across the grain of the meat into thin strips, approximately ¼ × 2 inches
- ½ cup dry red wine
- 1 small onion, chopped
- 2 carrots, peeled and thinly sliced
- 3 2 plum tomatoes, chopped
- 1 celery stalk, chopped
- 1 10-ounce package frozen peas
- 3 garlic gloves, minced
- 1 tablespoon Dijon mustard
- ½ teaspoon ground cumin
- ½ teaspoon dried tarragon
- Salt and freshly ground black pepper to taste

Directions:

1. Preheat the toaster oven to 375° F.
2. Combine all the ingredients with ½ cup water in an 8½ × 8½ × 4-inch ovenproof baking dish. Adjust the seasonings. Cover with aluminum foil.
3. BAKE, covered, for 45 minutes, or until the beef, onion, and celery are tender. Remove the cover.
4. BROIL 8 minutes to reduce the liquid and lightly brown the top.

Kashaburgers

Servings: 4

Cooking Time: 50 Minutes

Ingredients:

- 1 cup kasha
- 2 tablespoons minced onion or scallions
- 1 tablespoon minced garlic
- ½ cup multigrain bread crumbs
- 1 egg
- ¼ teaspoon paprika
- ½ teaspoon chili powder
- ¼ teaspoon sesame oil
- 1 tablespoon vegetable oil
- Salt and freshly ground black pepper to taste

Directions:

1. Preheat the toaster oven to 400° F.
2. Combine 2 cups water and the kasha in a 1-quart 8½ × 8½ × 4-inch ovenproof baking dish.
3. BAKE, uncovered, for 30 minutes, or until the grains are cooked. Remove from the oven and add all the other ingredients, stirring to mix well. When the mixture is cooled, shape into 4 to 6 patties and place on a rack with a broiling pan underneath.
4. BROIL for 20 minutes, turn with a spatula, then broil for another 10 minutes, or until browned.

Crab Chowder

Servings: 4
Cooking Time: 40 Minutes

Ingredients:

- 1 6-ounce can lump crabmeat, drained and chopped, or ½ pound fresh crabmeat, cleaned and chopped
- 1 cup skim milk or low-fat soy milk
- 1 cup fat-free half-and-half
- 2 tablespoons unbleached flour
- ¼ cup chopped onion
- ½ cup peeled and diced potato
- 1 carrot, peeled and chopped
- 1 celery stalk, chopped
- 2 garlic cloves, minced
- 2 tablespoons chopped fresh parsley
- ½ teaspoon ground cumin
- 1 teaspoon paprika
- Salt and butcher's pepper to taste

Directions:

1. Preheat the toaster oven to 400° F.
2. Whisk together the milk, half-and-half, and flour in a bowl. Transfer the mixture to a 1-quart 8½ × 8½ × 4-inch ovenproof baking dish. Add all the other ingredients, mixing well. Adjust the seasonings to taste.
3. BAKE, covered, for 40 minutes, or until the vegetables are tender.

Connecticut Garden Chowder

Servings: 4
Cooking Time: 60 Minutes

Ingredients:

- Soup:
- ½ cup peeled and shredded potato
- ½ cup shredded carrot
- ½ cup shredded celery 2 plum tomatoes, chopped
- 1 small zucchini, shredded
- 2 bay leaves
- ¼ teaspoon sage
- 1 teaspoon garlic powder
- Salt and butcher's pepper to taste
- Chowder base:
- 2 tablespoons reduced-fat cream cheese, at room temperature
- ½ cup fat-free half-and-half
- 2 tablespoons unbleached flour
- 2 tablespoons chopped fresh parsley

Directions:

1. Preheat the toaster oven to 375° F.
2. Combine the soup ingredients in a 1-quart 8½ × 8½ × 4-inch ovenproof baking dish, mixing well. Adjust the seasonings to taste.
3. BAKE, covered, for 40 minutes, or until the vegetables are tender.
4. Whisk the chowder mixture ingredients together until smooth. Add the mixture to the cooked soup ingredients and stir well to blend.
5. BAKE, uncovered for 20 minutes, or until the stock is thickened. Ladle the soup into individual soup bowls and garnish with the parsley.

Very Quick Pizza

Servings: 1
Cooking Time: 3 Minutes

Ingredients:

- 2 tablespoons salsa
- 1 6-inch whole wheat pita bread
- 2 tablespoons shredded part-skim, low-moisture mozzarella cheese

Directions:

1. Spread the salsa on the pita bread and sprinkle with the cheese.
2. TOAST once, or until the cheese is melted.

Meat Lovers Pan Pizza

Servings: 9
Cooking Time: 15 Minutes

Ingredients:

- Dough
- ¾ cup plus 1½ tablespoons warm water, 100°-110°F
- 1¾ teaspoons instant yeast
- 2 cups all-purpose flour, plus more for dusting
- 1 teaspoon kosher salt
- 1 tablespoon extra virgin olive oil, plus more for drizzling
- Toppings
- 6 tablespoons pizza sauce
- 8 ounces shredded low-moisture mozzarella
- Pepperoni slices
- 8 ounces cooked Italian sausage
- Crushed red pepper, for sprinkling
- Dried oregano, for sprinkling
- Black pepper, for sprinkling

Directions:

1. Pour water into a large mixing bowl, then whisk in the yeast. Allow to bloom for 10 minutes.
2. Add the flour and salt and mix with your hands until no dry flour remains.
3. Cover the dough tightly with plastic wrap and allow to rest at room temperature for 15 hours.
4. Add the olive oil and form into a ball.
5. Drizzle extra-virgin olive oil generously on the food tray and use your hands to coat evenly.
6. Place the dough on the food tray and spread it out slightly toward the corners of the pan.
7. Drizzle some more extra-virgin olive oil on top and use your hands to evenly coat the top of the dough.
8. Cover the dough and allow it to rest for 90 minutes.
9. Spread the dough out further so that it covers the bottom of the pan, then pop any bubbles that formed in the dough.
10. Spread pizza sauce on the dough, followed by cheese, then pepperoni and sausage.
11. Sprinkle the pizza with crushed red pepper, dried oregano, and black pepper.
12. Preheat the toaster Oven to 450°F.
13. Insert the pizza at low position in the preheated oven.
14. Select the Pizza function, adjust time to 15 minutes, and press Start/Pause.
15. Remove when done and allow to rest for 5 minutes before cutting.
16. Cut the pizza into squares and serve.

Rosemary Lentils

Servings: 2
Cooking Time: 35 Minutes

Ingredients:
- ¼ cup lentils
- 1 tablespoon mashed Roasted Garlic
- 1 rosemary sprig
- 1 bay leaf
- Salt and freshly ground black pepper
- 2 tablespoons low-fat buttermilk
- 2 tablespoons tomato sauce

Directions:
1. Preheat the toaster oven to 400° F.
2. Combine the lentils, 1¼ cups water, garlic, rosemary sprig, and bay leaf in a 1-quart 8½ × 8½ × 4-inch ovenproof baking dish, stirring to blend well. Add the salt and pepper to taste. Cover with aluminum foil.
3. BAKE, covered, for 35 minutes, or until the lentils are tender. Remove the rosemary sprig and bay leaf and stir in the buttermilk and tomato sauce. Serve immediately.

Baked Parsleyed Cheese Grits

Servings: 4
Cooking Time: 30 Minutes

Ingredients:
- 4 strips lean uncooked turkey bacon, cut in half
- 1 cup grits
- 2 cups skim or low-fat soy milk
- 1 egg
- ½ cup shredded Parmesan cheese
- 1 tablespoon chopped fresh parsley
- ½ teaspoon garlic powder
- Salt and butcher's pepper to taste

Directions:
1. Preheat the toaster oven to 350° F.
2. Layer an 8½ × 8½ × 2-inch square baking (cake) pan with the bacon strips.
3. Combine the remaining ingredients in a medium bowl and pour the mixture over the strips.
4. BAKE, uncovered, for 30 minutes, or until the grits are cooked. Cut into squares with a spatula and serve.

Pesto Pizza

Servings: 1

Cooking Time: 20 Minutes

Ingredients:

- Topping:
- ½ cup chopped fresh basil
- 1 tablespoon pine nuts (pignoli)
- 1 tablespoon olive oil
- 2 tablespoons shredded Parmesan cheese
- 1 garlic clove, minced
- ½ teaspoon dried oregano or 1 tablespoon chopped fresh oregano
- 1 plum tomato, chopped
- Salt and pepper to taste
- 1 9-inch ready-made pizza crust
- 2 tablespoons shredded low-fat mozzarella

Directions:

1. Preheat the toaster oven to 375° F.

2. Combine the topping ingredients in a small bowl.

3. Process the mixture in a blender or food processor until smooth. Spread the mixture on the pizza crust, then sprinkle with the mozzarella cheese. Place the pizza crust on the toaster oven rack.

4. BAKE for 20 minutes, or until the cheese is melted and the crust is brown.

Roasted Harissa Chicken + Vegetables

Servings: 4
Cooking Time: 30 Minutes

Ingredients:

- Nonstick cooking spray
- 1 medium zucchini, halved lengthwise and sliced crosswise ½ inch thick
- ½ large red onion, sliced ¼ inch thick
- 2 tablespoons olive oil
- Kosher salt and freshly ground black pepper
- 1 pound boneless, skinless chicken breasts, cut into 1-inch cubes
- ½ teaspoon ground cumin
- 1 clove garlic, minced
- 2 tablespoons harissa sauce or paste
- 1 tablespoon honey
- 2 tablespoons minced fresh cilantro
- 2 cups hot cooked rice
- Optional toppings: plain Greek yogurt or sour cream, sesame seeds (toasted or chopped), or dry-roasted peanuts

Directions:

1. Preheat the toaster oven to 400°F. Spray a 12 x 12-inch baking pan with nonstick cooking spray.

2. Place the zucchini and red onion in a medium bowl. Drizzle with 1 tablespoon olive oil and season with salt and pepper. Stir to coat the vegetables evenly. Arrange the vegetables in a single layer in the prepared baking pan. Roast, uncovered, for 10 minutes.

3. Place the chicken cubes in that same bowl. Drizzle with the remaining 1 tablespoon olive oil. Season with the cumin, garlic, salt, and pepper. Stir to coat the chicken evenly.

4. Stir the vegetables and move to one side of the pan. Arrange the chicken in a single layer on the other side of the pan. Roast for 10 minutes.

5. Blend the harissa and honey in a small bowl. Drizzle the sauce over the chicken and vegetables. Using a pastry brush, coat the chicken and vegetables evenly. Roast, uncovered, for an additional 8 to 10 minutes, or until the vegetables are tender and the chicken registers 165°F on a meat thermometer.

6. Spoon the chicken, vegetables, and any collected liquid onto a serving platter. Sprinkle with the cilantro. Serve the chicken and vegetables with the rice and, if desired, a dollop of plain Greek yogurt and a sprinkling of sesame seeds.

Chicken Noodle Soup

Servings: 4

Cooking Time: 45 Minutes

Ingredients:

- 1 cup egg noodles, uncooked
- 1 skinless, boneless chicken breast filet, cut into 1-inch pieces
- 1 carrot, peeled and chopped
- 1 celery stalk, chopped
- 1 plum tomato, chopped
- 1 small onion, peeled and chopped
- 1 tablespoon chopped fresh parsley
- 1 teaspoon dried basil
- Salt and freshly ground black pepper to taste

Directions:

1. Preheat the toaster oven to 400° F.
2. Combine all the ingredients with 3 cups water in a 1-quart 8½ × 8½ × 4-inch ovenproof baking dish.
3. BAKE, covered, for 45 minutes, or until the vegetables and chicken are tender.

Classic Potato Chips

Servings: 4
Cooking Time: 8 Minutes

Ingredients:

- 2 medium russet potatoes, washed
- 2 cups filtered water
- 1 tablespoon avocado oil
- ½ teaspoon salt

Directions:

1. Using a mandolin, slice the potatoes into ⅛-inch-thick pieces.
2. Pour the water into a large bowl. Place the potatoes in the bowl and soak for at least 30 minutes.
3. Preheat the toaster oven to 350°F.
4. Drain the water and pat the potatoes dry with a paper towel or kitchen cloth. Toss with avocado oil and salt. Liberally spray the air fryer oven with olive oil mist.
5. Set the potatoes inside the air fryer oven, separating them so they're not on top of each other. Air-fry for 10 minutes, or until browned.
6. Remove and let cool a few minutes prior to serving. Repeat until all the chips are cooked.

Asparagus With Pistachio Dukkah

Servings: 3

Cooking Time: 8 Minutes

Ingredients:

- Pistachio Dukkah Ingredients
- 3 tablespoons coriander seeds
- 1 tablespoon cumin seeds
- ½ cup shelled pistachios
- ¼ cup sesame seeds
- 1 teaspoon salt
- ½ teaspoon pepper
- Asparagus Ingredients
- 1 bundle asparagus spears
- 1 tablespoon olive oil
- Salt & pepper, to taste

Directions:

1. Make the pistachio dukkah by placing the coriander and cumin seeds in a skillet over medium heat. Toast for 2 minutes, or until fragrant. Transfer spices to a spice grinder or mortar and pestle. Allow spices to cool completely, then grind.

2. Toast the pistachios in a skillet for 5 minutes, or until golden brown and fragrant. Transfer to a cutting board and chop finely. Add the sesame seeds to the same skillet and toast for 2 minutes, or until golden brown and

3. fragrant. Transfer the pistachios, sesame seeds, coriander, and cumin seeds to a bowl. Add salt and pepper, then stir to combine.

4. Select the Preheat function on the Cosori Smart Air Fryer Toaster Oven, adjust temperature to 430°F, and press Start/Pause.

5. Line the food tray with foil, then place the asparagus on the tray. Drizzle with olive oil and season with salt and pepper.

6. Insert food tray at top position in the preheated oven.

7. Select the Air Fry function, adjust time to 8 minutes, and press Start/Pause.

8. Remove when asparagus is tender. Place asparagus on a serving dish and sprinkle with pistachio dukkah.

9. Pistachio dukkah can be stored at room temperature in a sealed jar or container for up to 4 weeks.

Fried Apple Wedges

Servings: 4
Cooking Time: 9 Minutes

Ingredients:

- ¼ cup panko breadcrumbs
- ¼ cup pecans
- 1½ teaspoons cinnamon
- 1½ teaspoons brown sugar
- ¼ cup cornstarch
- 1 egg white
- 2 teaspoons water
- 1 medium apple
- oil for misting or cooking spray

Directions:

1. In a food processor, combine panko, pecans, cinnamon, and brown sugar. Process to make small crumbs.
2. Place cornstarch in a plastic bag or bowl with lid. In a shallow dish, beat together the egg white and water until slightly foamy.
3. Preheat the toaster oven to 390°F.
4. Cut apple into small wedges. The thickest edge should be no more than ⅜- to ½-inch thick. Cut away the core, but do not peel.
5. Place apple wedges in cornstarch, reseal bag or bowl, and shake to coat.
6. Dip wedges in egg wash, shake off excess, and roll in crumb mixture. Spray with oil.
7. Place apples in air fryer oven in single layer and air-fry for 5 minutes.Break apart any apples that have stuck together. Mist lightly with oil and cook 4 minutes longer, until crispy.

Skinny Fries

Servings: 2
Cooking Time: 15 Minutes

Ingredients:

- 2 to 3 russet potatoes, peeled and cut into ¼-inch sticks
- 2 to 3 teaspoons olive or vegetable oil
- salt

Directions:

1. Cut the potatoes into ¼-inch strips. (A mandolin with a julienne blade is really helpful here.) Rinse the potatoes with cold water several times and let them soak in cold water for at least 10 minutes or as long as overnight.
2. Preheat the toaster oven to 380°F.
3. Drain and dry the potato sticks really well, using a clean kitchen towel. Toss the fries with the oil in a bowl and then air-fry the fries in two batches at 380°F for 15 minutes.
4. Add the first batch of French fries back into the air fryer oven with the finishing batch and let everything warm through for a few minutes. As soon as the fries are done, season them with salt and transfer to a plate. Serve them warm with ketchup or your favorite dip.

Baked Spicy Pimento Cheese Dip

Servings: 20

Cooking Time: 45 Minutes

Ingredients:

- 1 jar (4 oz.) sweet pimentos, drained
- 8 ounces block of cheddar cheese, shredded
- 2 Tablespoons hot sauce
- 2 teaspoons jarred garlic (or 2 whole cloves)
- 1/4 cup chopped onion
- 1/2 cup mayonnaise
- 1/2 teaspoon salt
- 1/2 teaspoon pepper
- 8 ounces cream cheese

Directions:

1. Preheat toaster oven to 350 degrees.
2. Combine all ingredients in a large bowl, then mix well using a hand blender, food processor or hand mixer.
3. Transfer cheese mixture into a shallow metal baking dish (8x8).
4. Place into toaster oven and bake for 40-45 minutes, or until edges are golden brown and bubbling.

Homemade Pretzel Bites

Servings: 8
Cooking Time: 6 Minutes

Ingredients:
- 4¾ cups filtered water, divided
- 1 tablespoon butter
- 1 package fast-rising yeast
- ½ teaspoon salt
- 2⅓ cups bread flour
- 2 tablespoons baking soda
- 2 egg whites
- 1 teaspoon kosher salt

Directions:
1. Preheat the toaster oven to 370°F.
2. In a large microwave-safe bowl, add ¾ cup of the water. Heat for 40 seconds in the microwave. Remove and whisk in the butter; then mix in the yeast and salt. Let sit 5 minutes.
3. Using a stand mixer with a dough hook attachment, add the yeast liquid and mix in the bread flour ⅓ cup at a time until all the flour is added and a dough is formed.
4. Remove the bowl from the stand; then let the dough rise 1 hour in a warm space, covered with a kitchen towel.
5. After the dough has doubled in size, remove from the bowl and punch down a few times on a lightly floured flat surface.
6. Divide the dough into 4 balls; then roll each ball out into a long, skinny, sticklike shape. Using a sharp knife, cut each dough stick into 6 pieces.
7. Repeat Step 6 for the remaining dough balls until you have about 24 bites formed.
8. Heat the remaining 4 cups of water over the stovetop in a medium pot with the baking soda stirred in.
9. Drop the pretzel bite dough into the hot water and let boil for 60 seconds, remove, and let slightly cool.
10. Lightly brush the top of each bite with the egg whites, and then cover with a pinch of kosher salt.
11. Spray the air fryer oven with olive oil spray and place the pretzel bites on top. Air-fry for 6 to 8 minutes, or until lightly browned. Remove and keep warm.
12. Repeat until all pretzel bites are cooked.
13. Serve warm.

Sweet Apple Fries

Servings: 3

Cooking Time: 8 Minutes

Ingredients:

- 2 Medium-size sweet apple(s), such as Gala or Fuji
- 1 Large egg white(s)
- 2 tablespoons Water
- 1½ cups Finely ground gingersnap crumbs (gluten-free, if a concern)
- Vegetable oil spray

Directions:

1. Preheat the toaster oven to 375°F .
2. Peel and core an apple, then cut it into 12 slices . Repeat with more apples as necessary.
3. Whisk the egg white(s) and water in a medium bowl until foamy. Add the apple slices and toss well to coat.
4. Spread the gingersnap crumbs across a dinner plate. Using clean hands, pick up an apple slice, let any excess egg white mixture slip back into the rest, and dredge the slice in the crumbs, coating it lightly but evenly on all sides. Set it aside and continue coating the remaining apple slices.
5. Lightly coat the slices on all sides with vegetable oil spray, then set them curved side down in the air fryer oven in one layer. Air-fry undisturbed for 6 minutes, or until browned and crisp. You may need to air-fry the slices for 2 minutes longer if the temperature is at 360°F.
6. Use kitchen tongs to transfer the slices to a wire rack. Cool for 2 to 3 minutes before serving.

Fried Green Tomatoes

Servings: 4

Cooking Time: 15 Minutes

Ingredients:

- 2 eggs
- ¼ cup buttermilk
- ½ cup cornmeal
- ½ cup breadcrumbs
- ¼ teaspoon salt
- 1½ pounds firm green tomatoes, cut in ¼-inch slices
- oil for misting or cooking spray
- Horseradish Drizzle
- ¼ cup mayonnaise
- ¼ cup sour cream
- 2 teaspoons prepared horseradish
- ½ teaspoon Worcestershire sauce
- ½ teaspoon lemon juice
- ⅛ teaspoon black pepper

Directions:

1. Mix all ingredients for Horseradish Drizzle together and chill while you prepare the green tomatoes.
2. Preheat the toaster oven to 390°F.
3. Beat the eggs and buttermilk together in a shallow bowl.
4. Mix cornmeal, breadcrumbs, and salt together in a plate or shallow dish.
5. Dip 4 tomato slices in the egg mixture, then roll in the breadcrumb mixture.
6. Mist one side with oil and place in air fryer oven, oil-side down, in a single layer.
7. Mist the top with oil.
8. Air-fry for 15 minutes, turning once, until brown and crispy.
9. Repeat steps 5 through 8 to cook remaining tomatoes.
10. Drizzle horseradish sauce over tomatoes just before serving.

Sweet Plantain Chips

Servings: 4

Cooking Time: 11 Minutes

Ingredients:

- 2 Very ripe plantain(s), peeled and sliced into 1-inch pieces
- Vegetable oil spray
- 3 tablespoons Maple syrup
- For garnishing Coarse sea salt or kosher salt

Directions:

1. Pour about ½ cup water into the bottom of your air fryer oven or into a metal tray on a lower rack in some models. Preheat the toaster oven to 400°F.

2. Put the plantain pieces in a bowl, coat them with vegetable oil spray, and toss gently, spraying at least one more time and tossing repeatedly, until the pieces are well coated.

3. When the machine is at temperature, arrange the plantain pieces in the air fryer oven in one layer. Air-fry undisturbed for 5 minutes.

4. Remove the pan from the machine and spray the back of a metal spatula with vegetable oil spray. Use the spatula to press down on the plantain pieces, spraying it again as needed, to flatten the pieces to about half their original height. Brush the plantain pieces with maple syrup, then return the pan to the machine and continue air-frying undisturbed for 6 minutes, or until the plantain pieces are soft and caramelized.

5. Use kitchen tongs to transfer the pieces to a serving platter. Sprinkle the pieces with salt and cool for a couple of minutes before serving. Or cool to room temperature before serving, about 1 hour.

Rosemary Roasted Vegetables

Servings: 4

Cooking Time: 25 Minutes

Ingredients:

- 3 tablespoons olive oil
- Grated zest and juice of 1 lemon
- 2 tablespoons chopped fresh rosemary leaves
- 4 cloves garlic, minced
- Kosher salt and freshly ground black pepper
- 6 cups vegetables, diced, such as bell peppers, onions, zucchini, mushrooms, cherry tomatoes, potatoes, and eggplant

Directions:

1. Preheat the toaster oven to 425 ºF.

2. Stir the olive oil, lemon zest, lemon juice, rosemary, and garlic in a small bowl. Season with salt and pepper. Place the vegetables into a large bowl and drizzle the olive oil mixture over all. Stir gently to coat.

3. Arrange the vegetables in a single layer in a 12 x 12-inch baking pan. Roast for 10 minutes. Stir and roast for an additional 10 to 15 minutes, or until the vegetables are tender.

Breaded Zucchini

Servings: 4
Cooking Time: 10 Minutes

Ingredients:

- 1 cup all-purpose flour
- 2 large eggs
- 1½ cups panko bread crumbs
- ½ cup grated Parmesan cheese
- Sea salt, for seasoning
- Freshly ground black pepper, for seasoning
- Oil spray (hand-pumped)
- 2 zucchini, cut into ¼-inch slices

Directions:

1. Preheat the toaster oven on AIR FRY to 350°F for 5 minutes.

2. Sprinkle the flour onto a plate.

3. In a small bowl, beat the eggs and place the bowl next to the flour.

4. In a medium bowl, stir the bread crumbs and cheese and season the mixture with salt and pepper. Place the bowl next to the eggs.

5. Place the air-fryer basket on the baking sheet and generously spray the rack with oil.

6. Dredge a zucchini slice in the flour, then the eggs, then the bread crumb mixture until well coated. Place the slice in the basket and repeat with the remaining zucchini slices. Spray the slices on both sides with oil.

7. In position 2, air fry for 10 minutes, turning once at 5 minutes, until golden brown and crispy. Serve immediately.

Foolproof Baked White Rice

Servings: 2
Cooking Time: 45 Minutes

Ingredients:

- 1¾ cups boiling water
- 1 cup long-grain white rice, rinsed
- 1 teaspoon extra-virgin olive oil
- ¼ teaspoon table salt

Directions:

1. Adjust toaster oven rack to middle position and preheat the toaster oven to 450 degrees. Combine all ingredients in 8-inch square baking dish or pan. Cover dish tightly with aluminum foil and bake until liquid is absorbed and rice is tender, 20 to 30 minutes, rotating dish halfway through baking.

2. Remove dish from oven, uncover, and fluff rice with fork, scraping up any rice that has stuck to bottom. Re-cover dish with foil and let rice sit for 10 minutes. Season with salt and pepper to taste. Serve.

Broiled Maryland Crabcakes With Creamy Herb Sauce

Servings: 8-9

Cooking Time: 8 Minutes

Ingredients:

- 1 large egg
- 3 Tablespoons mayonnaise
- 1 Tablespoon brown mustard
- 1 Tablespoon all-purpose flour
- 1 teaspoon seafood seasoning
- 1/2 teasoon salt
- 1/4 teaspoon ground black pepper
- 1 pound lump crabmeat
- 1/4 cup chopped parsley
- 1 small shallot, minced
- 1 garlic clove, minced
- Creamy Herb Sauce

Directions:

1. In a medium bowl, mix egg, mayonnaise, mustard, flour, seafood seasoning, salt and pepper until well blended.

2. Stir in crabmeat, parsley, shallots and garlic until crab is coated with mayonnaise mixture.

3. Place 1/4 cup crab mixture on broiler pan; lightly press down. Repeat with remaining mixture.

4. Set toaster oven on BROIL. Broil crabcakes 8 minutes, without turning.

5. Serve with Creamy Herb Sauce.

Creamy Parmesan Polenta

Servings: 4

Cooking Time: 60 Minutes

Ingredients:

- 2½ cups boiling water, divided, plus extra as needed
- ½ cup coarse-ground cornmeal
- ½ teaspoon table salt
- Pinch baking soda
- 1 ounce Parmesan cheese, grated (½ cup)
- 1 tablespoon unsalted butter

Directions:

1. Adjust toaster oven rack to middle position and preheat the toaster oven to 325 degrees. Combine 2 cups boiling water, cornmeal, salt, and baking soda in greased 8-inch square baking dish or pan. Transfer dish to oven and bake until water is absorbed and polenta is thickened, 35 to 40 minutes, rotating dish halfway through baking.

2. Remove baking dish from oven. Stir in remaining ½ cup boiling water, then stir in Parmesan and butter until polenta is smooth and creamy. Adjust consistency with extra boiling water as needed. Serve.

Mozzarella-stuffed Arancini

Servings: 14

Cooking Time: 20 Minutes

Ingredients:

- Pie Crust
- 3½ cups low sodium chicken stock
- 4 tablespoons unsalted butter, divided
- 1 medium onion, finely chopped
- 2 garlic cloves, minced
- 1 cup arborio rice
- 1½ teaspoons kosher salt, plus more to taste
- ½ cup dry white wine
- 2 ounces finely grated Parmesan
- ¼ cup heavy cream
- 1 teaspoon freshly ground black pepper, plus more to taste
- 3 ounces low-moisture mozzarella, cut into ⅓-inch pieces
- 1½ cups panko breadcrumbs
- 2 tablespoons melted salted butter
- ½ cup all-purpose flour 2 large eggs, beaten Cooking spray
- Marinara sauce, for serving

Directions:

1. Simmer chicken stock in a pot, then keep warm on low heat.
2. Heat 2 tablespoons of unsalted butter in a medium saucepan over medium heat.
3. Add onions to the saucepan and cook for 5 minutes or until softened.
4. Add garlic and cook for 1 minute or until softened.
5. Add rice and 1½ teaspoons of kosher salt to the saucepan.
6. Cook the rice for 3 minutes or until the edges turn translucent.
7. Pour in the wine, stir, and cook for 3 minutes or until the wine is all evaporated and the rice looks dry.
8. Ladle in 1 cup of the warm chicken stock and bring to a simmer. Stirring often, cook the rice for 5 minutes or until liquid is absorbed. Repeat this process with another cup of chicken stock.
9. Add the remaining 1½ cups of chicken stock and cook, stirring often, for 10 minutes or until the rice is cooked through but toothsome and the liquid is mostly absorbed.
10. Remove the risotto from the heat and mix in Parmesan, heavy cream, black pepper, and the remaining two tablespoons of unsalted butter.
11. Season the risotto to taste with salt and black pepper.
12. Spread risotto in an even layer on a parchment-lined baking sheet and cover with plastic wrap.
13. Place the risotto in the fridge and chill for 4 hours.
14. Seperate the chilled risotto into 14 even pieces and form them into round patties about 2½ inches in diameter.
15. Place a piece of mozzarella in the center of a patty, pinch and shape the risotto so it completely encases the cheese, then roll into a ball. Repeat with each risotto patty.
16. Place the balls onto the baking sheet lined with fresh parchment paper, cover with plastic wrap, and place in the freezer for 15 minutes.

17. Place the panko breadcrumbs into a food processor and pulse until finely ground, then place into a bowl.
18. Mix the panko breadcrumbs with the melted salted butter until well combined.
19. Remove the risotto balls from the freezer and dredge in flour, dip in beaten eggs, then cover with breadcrumbs. Repeat this process with the rest of the balls. Set aside.
20. Preheat the toaster oven to 400°F.
21. Place the balls into the fry basket, spray them liberally with cooking spray, then insert the basket at mid position in the preheated oven.
22. Select the Air Fry function, adjust time to 20 minutes, and press Start/Pause.
23. Remove the arancini from the oven and serve with marinara sauce.

Sweet Chili– Glazed Wings

Servings: 4

Cooking Time: 27 Minutes

Ingredients:

- 1 pound chicken wing drumettes
- ½ cup reduced-sodium soy sauce
- 3 tablespoons honey
- 3 tablespoons unseasoned rice vinegar
- 1 tablespoon sesame oil
- 1 ½ teaspoons chili garlic paste
- ¼ teaspoon freshly ground black pepper
- ¼ cup jarred Asian sweet chili sauce

Directions:

1. Place the chicken drumettes in a deep bowl. Stir the soy sauce, honey, rice vinegar, sesame oil, chili garlic paste, and pepper in a small bowl. Pour the soy sauce mixture over the chicken. Cover the bowl and refrigerate for several hours or overnight.

2. Preheat the toaster oven to 375°F. Line a 12 x 12-inch baking pan with aluminum foil.

3. Drain and discard the marinade. Pat the chicken dry and arrange in a single layer in the prepared pan. Bake, uncovered, for 18 to 20 minutes or until lightly browned and almost done.

4. Brush the chicken with the sweet chili sauce, turning to coat evenly. Bake for 6 to 7 minutes or until the chicken is done, a meat thermometer registers 165°F, and the edges are beginning to crisp.

Cinnamon Pita Chips

Servings: 4

Cooking Time: 6 Minutes

Ingredients:

- 2 tablespoons sugar
- 2 teaspoons cinnamon
- 2 whole 6-inch pitas, whole grain or white
- oil for misting or cooking spray

Directions:

1. Mix sugar and cinnamon together.

2. Cut each pita in half and each half into 4 wedges. Break apart each wedge at the fold.

3. Mist one side of pita wedges with oil or cooking spray. Sprinkle them all with half of the cinnamon sugar.

4. Turn the wedges over, mist the other side with oil or cooking spray, and sprinkle with the remaining cinnamon sugar.

5. Place pita wedges in air fryer oven and air-fry at 330°F for 2 minutes.

6. Cook 2 more minutes. If needed cook 2 more minutes, until crisp. Watch carefully because at this point they will cook very quickly.

Panko-breaded Onion Rings

Servings: 4

Cooking Time: 12 Minutes

Ingredients:

- 1 large sweet onion, cut into ½-inch slices and rings separated
- 2 cups ice water
- ½ cup all-purpose flour
- 1 teaspoon paprika
- 1 teaspoon salt
- ½ teaspoon black pepper
- ½ teaspoon garlic powder
- ¼ teaspoon onion powder
- 1 egg, whisked
- 2 tablespoons milk
- 1 cup breadcrumbs

Directions:

1. Preheat the toaster oven to 400°F.
2. In a large bowl, soak the onion rings in the water for 5 minutes. Drain and pat dry with a towel.
3. In a medium bowl, place the flour, paprika, salt, pepper, garlic powder, and onion powder.
4. In a second bowl, whisk together the egg and milk.
5. In a third bowl, place the breadcrumbs.
6. To bread the onion rings, dip them first into the flour mixture, then into the egg mixture (shaking off the excess), and then into the breadcrumbs. Place the coated onion rings onto a plate while you bread all the rings.
7. Place the onion rings into the air fryer oven in a single layer, sometimes nesting smaller rings into larger rings. Spray with cooking spray. Air-fry for 3 minutes, turn the rings over, and spray with more cooking spray. Air-fry for another 3 to 5 minutes. Cook the rings in batches; you may need to do 2 or 3 batches, depending on the size of your air fryer oven.

Pork Belly Scallion Yakitori

Servings: 3

Cooking Time: 10 Minutes

Ingredients:

- ¼ cup soy sauce
- 1 tablespoons sake
- 2 tablespoons mirin
- 2 teaspoons rice wine vinegar
- 2 tablespoons dark brown sugar
- ½ teaspoon onion powder
- ¼ teaspoon garlic powder
- ¼ teaspoon kosher salt
- 1½ inch piece of ginger, peeled and roughly sliced
- 1 pound of ½-inch thick sliced pork belly, cut into 2-inch pieces
- 6 scallions
- Lemon wedges, for serving

Directions:

1. Combine soy sauce, sake, mirin, rice wine vinegar, dark brown sugar, onion powder, garlic powder, kosher salt, and ginger in a bowl.
2. Add the pork belly to the marinade and massage the marinade into the meat.
3. Cover and place into the refrigerator for 5 hours.
4. Remove from the fridge and pat the pork belly dry with paper towels. Set aside and allow to sit at room temperature for 1 hour.
5. Cut off the thinner dark green part of the scallion and discard.
6. Cut the trimmed scallions into thirds.
7. Skewer a piece of pork belly, followed by a piece of scallion, then repeat until the skewer is filled. Place the skewers onto the food tray.
8. Preheat the toaster oven to 450°F.
9. Insert the food tray with yakitori at top position in the preheated oven.
10. Select the Broil and Shake functions, then press Start/Pause.
11. Flip the yakitori halfway through cooking. The Shake Reminder will let you know when.
12. Remove when done and serve with a wedge of lemon.

FISH AND SEAFOOD

Bacon-wrapped Scallops

Servings: 4
Cooking Time: 8 Minutes

Ingredients:

- 16 large scallops
- 8 bacon strips
- ½ teaspoon black pepper
- ¼ teaspoon smoked paprika

Directions:

1. Pat the scallops dry with a paper towel. Slice each of the bacon strips in half. Wrap 1 bacon strip around 1 scallop and secure with a toothpick. Repeat with the remaining scallops. Season the scallops with pepper and paprika.

2. Preheat the toaster oven to 350°F.

3. Place the bacon-wrapped scallops in the air fryer oven and air-fry for 4 minutes. Cook another 6 to 7 minutes. When the bacon is crispy, the scallops should be cooked through and slightly firm, but not rubbery. Serve immediately.

Better Fish Sticks

Servings: 3
Cooking Time: 8 Minutes

Ingredients:

- ¾ cup Seasoned Italian-style dried bread crumbs (gluten-free, if a concern)
- 3 tablespoons (about ½ ounce) Finely grated Parmesan cheese
- 10 ounces Skinless cod fillets, cut lengthwise into 1-inch-wide pieces
- 3 tablespoons Regular or low-fat mayonnaise (not fat-free; gluten-free, if a concern)
- Vegetable oil spray

Directions:

1. Preheat the toaster oven to 400°F.

2. Mix the bread crumbs and grated Parmesan in a shallow soup bowl or a small pie plate.

3. Smear the fish fillet sticks completely with the mayonnaise, then dip them one by one in the bread-crumb mixture, turning and pressing gently to make an even and thorough coating. Coat each stick on all sides with vegetable oil spray.

4. Set the fish sticks in the air fryer oven with at least ¼ inch between them. Air-fry undisturbed for 8 minutes, or until golden brown and crisp.

5. Use a nonstick-safe spatula to gently transfer them from the air fryer oven to a wire rack. Cool for only a minute or two before serving.

Mediterranean Baked Fish

Servings: 4

Cooking Time: 25 Minutes

Ingredients:

- Baking mixture:
- 1 tablespoon olive oil
- 2 tablespoons tomato paste
- 3 plum tomatoes, chopped
- 2 garlic cloves, minced
- 2 tablespoons capers
- 2 tablespoons pitted and chopped black olives
- 2 tablespoons chopped fresh basil leaves
- 2 tablespoons chopped fresh parsley
- 4 6-ounce fish fillets (red snapper, cod, whiting, sole, or mackerel)

Directions:

1. Preheat the toaster oven to 350° F.

2. Combine the baking mixture ingredients in a small bowl. Set aside.

3. Layer the fillets in an oiled or nonstick 8½ × 8½ × 2-inch square baking (cake) pan, overlapping them if necessary, and spoon the baking mixture over the fish.

4. BAKE, covered, for 25 minutes, or until the fish flakes easily with a fork.

Miso-rubbed Salmon Fillets

Servings: 3

Cooking Time: 5 Minutes

Ingredients:

- ¼ cup White (shiro) miso paste (usually made from rice and soy beans)
- 1½ tablespoons Mirin or a substitute
- 2½ teaspoons Unseasoned rice vinegar
- Vegetable oil spray
- 3 6-ounce skin-on salmon fillets

Directions:

1. Preheat the toaster oven to 400°F.

2. Mix the miso, mirin, and vinegar in a small bowl until uniform.

3. Remove from the machine. Generously spray the skin side of each fillet. Pick them up one by one with a nonstick-safe spatula and set them in the baking pan skin side down with as much air space between them as possible. Coat the top of each fillet with the miso mixture, dividing it evenly between them.

4. Return the baking pan to the machine. Air-fry undisturbed for 5 minutes, or until lightly browned and firm.

5. Use a nonstick-safe spatula to transfer the fillets to serving plates. Cool for only a minute or so before serving.

Crunchy Clam Strips

Servings: 3
Cooking Time: 8 Minutes

Ingredients:

- ½ pound Clam strips, drained
- 1 Large egg, well beaten
- ½ cup All-purpose flour
- ½ cup Yellow cornmeal
- 1½ teaspoons Table salt
- 1½ teaspoons Ground black pepper
- Up to ¾ teaspoon Cayenne
- Vegetable oil spray

Directions:

1. Preheat the toaster oven to 400°F.
2. Toss the clam strips and beaten egg in a bowl until the clams are well coated.
3. Mix the flour, cornmeal, salt, pepper, and cayenne in a large zip-closed plastic bag until well combined. Using a flatware fork or small kitchen tongs, lift the clam strips one by one out of the egg, letting any excess egg slip back into the rest. Put the strips in the bag with the flour mixture. Once all the strips are in the bag, seal it until the strips are well coated.
4. Use kitchen tongs to pick out the clam strips and lay them on a cutting board (leaving any extra flour mixture in the bag to be discarded). Coat the strips on both sides with vegetable oil spray.
5. When the machine is at temperature, spread the clam strips in the air fryer oven in one layer. They may touch in places, but try to leave as much air space as possible around them. Air-fry undisturbed for 8 minutes, or until brown and crunchy.
6. Gently dump the contents of the air fryer oven onto a serving platter. Cool for just a minute or two before serving hot.

Baked Parsley Mussels With Zucchini

Servings: 6
Cooking Time: 40 Minutes

Ingredients:

- 2 pounds (approximately 40) mussels, cooked, shells discarded
- 4 small zucchini squash, scrubbed, halved, and cut lengthwise into ½-inch-wide strips
- ½ cup dry white wine
- 1 tablespoon chopped fresh oregano or 1 teaspoon dried oregano
- 2 garlic cloves, minced
- ¼ cup chopped fresh Italian parsley
- 2 tablespoons olive oil
- Freshly ground black pepper to taste
- ¼ cup grated low-fat Parmesan cheese

Directions:

1. Preheat the toaster oven to 350° F.
2. Combine all the ingredients except the Parmesan cheese in a 1-quart 8½ × 8½ × 4-inch ovenproof baking dish, mixing well. Adjust the seasonings to taste and cover with aluminum foil.
3. BAKE for 35 minutes, or until the zucchini is tender. Uncover and sprinkle with Parmesan cheese.
4. BROIL for 5 minutes, or until the cheese is melted and the top is lightly browned.

Tex-mex Fish Tacos

Servings: 3

Cooking Time: 7 Minutes

Ingredients:

- ¾ teaspoon Chile powder
- ¼ teaspoon Ground cumin
- ¼ teaspoon Dried oregano
- 3 5-ounce skinless mahi-mahi fillets
- Vegetable oil spray
- 3 Corn or flour tortillas
- 6 tablespoons Diced tomatoes
- 3 tablespoons Regular, low-fat, or fat-free sour cream

Directions:

1. Preheat the toaster oven to 400°F.

2. Stir the chile powder, cumin, and oregano in a small bowl until well combined.

3. Coat each piece of fish all over (even the sides and ends) with vegetable oil spray. Sprinkle the spice mixture evenly over all sides of the fillets. Lightly spray them again.

4. When the machine is at temperature, set the fillets in the air fryer oven with as much air space between them as possible. Air-fry undisturbed for 7 minutes, until lightly browned and firm but not hard.

5. Use a nonstick-safe spatula to transfer the fillets to a wire rack. Microwave the tortillas on high for a few seconds, until supple. Put a fillet in each tortilla and top each with 2 tablespoons diced tomatoes and 1 tablespoon sour cream.

Lobster Tails

Servings: 4

Cooking Time: 10 Minutes

Ingredients:

- Brushing mixture:
- 2 tablespoons lemon juice
- 2 tablespoons olive oil
- ½ teaspoon garlic powder
- ¼ teaspoon ground thyme
- 4 6-ounce lobster tails

Directions:

1. Whisk together the brushing mixture ingredients in a small bowl and set aside. CUT the top of each lobster shell lengthwise from the top edge to the tail with a sharp scissors. Place the lobster tails, cut side down, on a broiling rack with a pan underneath. Brush with the brushing mixture.

2. BROIL for 5 minutes. Remove from the oven and brush again. Broil for 5 minutes, or until the lobster flesh turns from translucent to opaque.

Tuna Nuggets In Hoisin Sauce

Servings: 4

Cooking Time: 7 Minutes

Ingredients:

- ½ cup hoisin sauce
- 2 tablespoons rice wine vinegar
- 2 teaspoons sesame oil
- 1 teaspoon garlic powder
- 2 teaspoons dried lemongrass
- ¼ teaspoon red pepper flakes
- ½ small onion, quartered and thinly sliced
- 8 ounces fresh tuna, cut into 1-inch cubes
- cooking spray
- 3 cups cooked jasmine rice

Directions:

1. Mix the hoisin sauce, vinegar, sesame oil, and seasonings together.
2. Stir in the onions and tuna nuggets.
3. Spray air fryer oven baking pan with nonstick spray and pour in tuna mixture.
4. Air-fry at 390°F for 3 minutes. Stir gently.
5. Cook 2 minutes and stir again, checking for doneness. Tuna should be barely cooked through, just beginning to flake and still very moist. If necessary, continue cooking and stirring in 1-minute intervals until done.
6. Serve warm over hot jasmine rice.

Coconut Jerk Shrimp

Servings: 3

Cooking Time: 8 Minutes

Ingredients:

- 1 Large egg white(s)
- 1 teaspoon Purchased or homemade jerk dried seasoning blend
- ¾ cup Plain panko bread crumbs (gluten-free, if a concern)
- ¾ cup Unsweetened shredded coconut
- 12 Large shrimp (20–25 per pound), peeled and deveined
- Coconut oil spray

Directions:

1. Preheat the toaster oven to 375°F .

2. Whisk the egg white(s) and seasoning blend in a bowl until foamy. Add the shrimp and toss well to coat evenly.

3. Mix the bread crumbs and coconut on a dinner plate until well combined. Use kitchen tongs to pick up a shrimp, letting the excess egg white mixture slip back into the rest. Set the shrimp in the bread-crumb mixture. Turn several times to coat evenly and thoroughly. Set on a cutting board and continue coating the remainder of the shrimp.

4. Lightly coat all the shrimp on both sides with the coconut oil spray. Set them in the air fryer oven in one layer with as much space between them as possible. (You can even stand some up along the air fryer oven's wall in some models.) Air-fry undisturbed for 6 minutes, or until the coating is lightly browned. If the air fryer oven is at 360°F, you may need to add 2 minutes to the cooking time.

5. Use clean kitchen tongs to transfer the shrimp to a wire rack. Cool for only a minute or two before serving.

Crispy Calamari

Servings: 4

Cooking Time: 30 Minutes

Ingredients:

- Oil spray (hand-pumped)
- ¾ cup buttermilk
- 1 large egg
- 1 cup panko bread crumbs
- ¾ cup all-purpose flour
- ½ teaspoon sea salt or Old Bay seasoning
- 1 pound frozen squid rings, thawed and drained well or fresh
- 1 lemon, cut into wedges

Directions:

1. Preheat the toaster oven to 400°F on AIR FRY for 5 minutes.
2. Place the air-fryer basket in the baking tray and generously spray it with the oil.
3. In a medium bowl, whisk the buttermilk and egg.
4. In another medium bowl, stir the bread crumbs, flour, and salt until well blended.
5. Dredge the squid in the buttermilk mixture and then dredge it in the bread crumb mixture.
6. Place the breaded calamari in the basket in a single layer and lightly spray it with the oil. You will have to do several batches.
7. In position 2, air fry for 10 minutes until crispy and golden brown. Cover the cooked calamari with foil to keep it warm while you cook the remaining batches.
8. Repeat with the remaining calamari rings.
9. Serve with lemon wedges.

Almond-crusted Fish

Servings: 4
Cooking Time: 10 Minutes

Ingredients:

- 4 4-ounce fish fillets
- ¾ cup breadcrumbs
- ¼ cup sliced almonds, crushed
- 2 tablespoons lemon juice
- ⅛ teaspoon cayenne
- salt and pepper
- ¾ cup flour
- 1 egg, beaten with 1 tablespoon water
- oil for misting or cooking spray

Directions:

1. Split fish fillets lengthwise down the center to create 8 pieces.
2. Mix breadcrumbs and almonds together and set aside.
3. Mix the lemon juice and cayenne together. Brush on all sides of fish.
4. Season fish to taste with salt and pepper.
5. Place the flour on a sheet of wax paper.
6. Roll fillets in flour, dip in egg wash, and roll in the crumb mixture.
7. Mist both sides of fish with oil or cooking spray.
8. Spray air fryer oven and lay fillets inside.
9. Air-fry at 390°F for 5 minutes, turn fish over, and air-fry for an additional 5 minutes or until fish is done and flakes easily.

Sweet Chili Shrimp

Servings: 4
Cooking Time: 6 Minutes

Ingredients:

- 1 pound jumbo shrimp, peeled and deveined
- ¼ cup sweet chili sauce
- 1 lime, zested and juiced
- 1 tablespoon soy sauce
- 1 tablespoon honey
- 1 tablespoon olive oil
- 1 large garlic clove, minced
- ½ teaspoon salt
- ¼ teaspoon pepper
- 1 green onion, thinly sliced, for garnish

Directions:

1. Place the shrimp in a large bowl. Whisk all the remaining ingredients except the green onion in a separate bowl.
2. Pour sauce over the shrimp and toss to coat.
3. Preheat the toaster Oven to 430°F.
4. Line the food tray with foil, place shrimp on the tray, then insert at top position in the preheated oven.
5. Select the Air Fry function, adjust time to 6 minutes, and press Start/Pause.
6. Remove shrimp and garnish with sliced green onions.

Fried Shrimp

Servings: 3

Cooking Time: 7 Minutes

Ingredients:

- 1 Large egg white
- 2 tablespoons Water
- 1 cup Plain dried bread crumbs (gluten-free, if a concern)
- ¼ cup All-purpose flour or almond flour
- ¼ cup Yellow cornmeal
- 1 teaspoon Celery salt
- 1 teaspoon Mild paprika
- Up to ½ teaspoon Cayenne (optional)
- ¾ pound Large shrimp (20–25 per pound), peeled and deveined
- Vegetable oil spray

Directions:

1. Preheat the toaster oven to 400°F.

2. Set two medium or large bowls on your counter. In the first, whisk the egg white and water until foamy. In the second, stir the bread crumbs, flour, cornmeal, celery salt, paprika, and cayenne (if using) until well combined.

3. Pour all the shrimp into the egg white mixture and stir gently until all the shrimp are coated. Use kitchen tongs to pick them up one by one and transfer them to the bread-crumb mixture. Turn each in the bread-crumb mixture to coat it evenly and thoroughly on all sides before setting it on a cutting board. When you're done coating the shrimp, coat them all on both sides with the vegetable oil spray.

4. Set the shrimp in as close to one layer in the air fryer oven as you can. Some may overlap. Air-fry for 7 minutes, gently rearranging the shrimp at the 4-minute mark to get covered surfaces exposed, until golden brown and firm but not hard.

5. Use kitchen tongs to gently transfer the shrimp to a wire rack. Cool for only a minute or two before serving.

Marinated Catfish

Servings: 4

Cooking Time: 10 Minutes

Ingredients:

- Marinade:
- 1 tablespoon olive oil
- 1 tablespoon lemon juice
- ¼ dry white wine
- 1 tablespoon garlic powder
- 1 tablespoon soy sauce
- 4 6-ounce catfish fillets

Directions:

1. Combine the marinade ingredients in an 8½ × 8½ × 4-inch ovenproof baking dish. Add the fillets and let stand for 10 minutes, spooning the marinade over the fillets every 2 minutes.

2. BROIL the fillets for 15 minutes, or until the fish flakes easily with a fork.

Shrimp With Jalapeño Dip

Servings: 4
Cooking Time: 10 Minutes

Ingredients:

- Seasonings:
- 1 teaspoon ground cumin
- 1 tablespoon minced garlic
- 1 teaspoon paprika
- 1 teaspoon chili powder
- Pinch of cayenne
- Salt to taste
- 1½ pounds large shrimp, peeled and deveined

Directions:

1. Combine the seasonings in a plastic bag, add the shrimp, and shake well to coat. Transfer the shrimp to an oiled or nonstick 8½ × 8½ × 2-inch square baking (cake) pan.
2. BROIL for 5 minutes. Remove the pan from the oven and turn the shrimp with tongs. Broil 5 minutes again, or until the shrimp are cooked (they should be firm but not rubbery.) Serve with Jalapeño Dip.

Halibut Tacos

Servings: 4
Cooking Time: 15 Minutes

Ingredients:

- Oil spray (hand-pumped)
- 1 teaspoon ground cumin
- ¼ teaspoon sea salt
- ⅛ teaspoon freshly ground black pepper
- 4 (4-ounce) halibut fillets
- 1 tablespoon olive oil
- 1 cup red cabbage, shredded
- 1 carrot, shredded
- 1 scallion, white and green parts, finely chopped
- ¼ cup sour cream
- Juice of 1 lime
- ⅛ teaspoon chili powder
- 4 (8-inch) corn tortillas, room temperature

Directions:

1. Preheat the toaster oven to 350°F on CONVECTION BAKE for 5 minutes.
2. Place the air-fryer basket in the baking tray and spray it generously with the oil.
3. In a small bowl, stir the cumin, salt, and pepper until well blended.
4. Season the fish all over with the seasoning mixture.
5. Place the fish in the basket and drizzle with the olive oil.
6. In position 2, bake for 15 minutes until cooked through and lightly browned.
7. While the fish is cooking, in a medium bowl, toss together the cabbage, carrot, scallion, sour cream, lime juice, and chili powder until very well mixed. Set aside.
8. Divide the fish among the tortillas and top with the slaw. Serve.

Garlic-lemon Shrimp Skewers

Servings: 2

Cooking Time: 8 Minutes

Ingredients:

- Juice and zest of 1 lemon
- 1 tablespoon olive oil
- ½ teaspoon garlic puree
- ¼ teaspoon smoked paprika
- 12 large shrimp, peeled and deveined
- Oil spray (hand-pumped)
- Sea salt, for seasoning
- Freshly ground black pepper, for seasoning
- 1 tablespoon chopped fresh parsley

Directions:

1. Preheat the toaster oven to 350°F on AIR FRY for 5 minutes.
2. In a medium bowl, stir the lemon juice, lemon zest, olive oil, garlic, and paprika.
3. Add the shrimp and toss to combine. Cover, refrigerate, and let marinate for 30 minutes.
4. Soak 4 wooden skewers in water while the shrimp marinate.
5. Place the air-fryer basket in the baking tray and spray it generously with the oil.
6. Thread 3 shrimp on each skewer and place them in the basket. Discard any remaining marinade.
7. In position 2, air fry for 8 minutes, turning halfway through, until just cooked.
8. Season with the salt and pepper and serve topped with the parsley.

Crispy Sweet-and-sour Cod Fillets

Servings: 3

Cooking Time: 12 Minutes

Ingredients:

- 1½ cups Plain panko bread crumbs (gluten-free, if a concern)
- 2 tablespoons Regular or low-fat mayonnaise (not fat-free; gluten-free, if a concern)
- ¼ cup Sweet pickle relish
- 3 4- to 5-ounce skinless cod fillets

Directions:

1. Preheat the toaster oven to 400°F.

2. Pour the bread crumbs into a shallow soup plate or a small pie plate. Mix the mayonnaise and relish in a small bowl until well combined. Smear this mixture all over the cod fillets. Set them in the crumbs and turn until evenly coated on all sides, even on the ends.

3. Set the coated cod fillets in the air fryer oven with as much air space between them as possible. They should not touch. Air-fry undisturbed for 12 minutes, or until browned and crisp.

4. Use a nonstick-safe spatula to transfer the cod pieces to a wire rack. Cool for only a minute or two before serving hot.

POULTRY

Crispy Duck With Cherry Sauce

Servings: 2

Cooking Time: 33 Minutes

Ingredients:

- 1 whole duck (up to 5 pounds), split in half, back and rib bones removed
- 1 teaspoon olive oil
- salt and freshly ground black pepper
- Cherry Sauce:
- 1 tablespoon butter
- 1 shallot, minced
- ½ cup sherry
- ¾ cup cherry preserves 1 cup chicken stock
- 1 teaspoon white wine vinegar
- 1 teaspoon fresh thyme leaves
- salt and freshly ground black pepper

Directions:

1. Preheat the toaster oven to 400°F.

2. Trim some of the fat from the duck. Rub olive oil on the duck and season with salt and pepper. Place the duck halves in the air fryer oven, breast side up and facing the center of the air fryer oven.

3. Air-fry the duck for 20 minutes. Turn the duck over and air-fry for another 6 minutes.

4. While duck is air-frying, make the cherry sauce. Melt the butter in a large sauté pan. Add the shallot and sauté until it is just starting to brown – about 2 to 3 minutes. Add the sherry and deglaze the pan by scraping up any brown bits from the bottom of the pan. Simmer the liquid for a few minutes, until it has reduced by half. Add the cherry preserves, chicken stock and white wine vinegar. Whisk well to combine all the ingredients. Simmer the sauce until it thickens and coats the back of a spoon – about 5 to 7 minutes. Season with salt and pepper and stir in the fresh thyme leaves.

5. When the air fryer oven timer goes off, spoon some cherry sauce over the duck and continue to air-fry at 400°F for 4 more minutes. Then, turn the duck halves back over so that the breast side is facing up. Spoon more cherry sauce over the top of the duck, covering the skin completely. Air-fry for 3 more minutes and then remove the duck to a plate to rest for a few minutes.

6. Serve the duck in halves, or cut each piece in half again for a smaller serving. Spoon any additional sauce over the duck or serve it on the side.

Chicken In Mango Sauce

Servings: 2

Cooking Time: 40 Minutes

Ingredients:

- 2 skinless and boneless chicken breast halves
- 1 tablespoon capers
- 1 tablespoon raisins
- Mango mixture:
- 1 cup mango pieces
- 1 teaspoon balsamic vinegar
- ½ teaspoon garlic powder
- 1 teaspoon fresh ginger, peeled and minced
- ½ teaspoon soy sauce
- ½ teaspoon curry powder
- 1 tablespoon pimientos, minced
- Salt and pepper to taste

Directions:

1. Preheat the toaster oven to 375° F.

2. Process the mango mixture ingredients in a food processor or blender until smooth. Transfer to an oiled or nonstick 8½ × 8½ × 2-inch square (cake) pan and add the capers, raisins, and pimientos, stirring well to blend. Add the chicken breasts and spoon the mixture over the breasts to coat well.

3. BAKE for 40 minutes. Serve the breasts with the sauce.

Chicken Schnitzel Dogs

Servings: 4

Cooking Time: 10 Minutes

Ingredients:

- ½ cup flour
- ½ teaspoon salt
- 1 teaspoon marjoram
- 1 teaspoon dried parsley flakes
- ½ teaspoon thyme
- 1 egg
- 1 teaspoon lemon juice
- 1 teaspoon water
- 1 cup breadcrumbs
- 4 chicken tenders, pounded thin
- oil for misting or cooking spray
- 4 whole-grain hotdog buns
- 4 slices Gouda cheese
- 1 small Granny Smith apple, thinly sliced
- ½ cup shredded Napa cabbage
- coleslaw dressing

Directions:

1. In a shallow dish, mix together the flour, salt, marjoram, parsley, and thyme.
2. In another shallow dish, beat together egg, lemon juice, and water.
3. Place breadcrumbs in a third shallow dish.
4. Cut each of the flattened chicken tenders in half lengthwise.
5. Dip flattened chicken strips in flour mixture, then egg wash. Let excess egg drip off and roll in breadcrumbs. Spray both sides with oil or cooking spray.
6. Air-fry at 390°F for 5 minutes. Spray with oil, turn over, and spray other side.
7. Air-fry for 3 to 5 minutes more, until well done and crispy brown.
8. To serve, place 2 schnitzel strips on bottom of each hot dog bun. Top with cheese, sliced apple, and cabbage. Drizzle with coleslaw dressing and top with other half of bun.

Chicken Fajitas

Servings: 4

Cooking Time: 15 Minutes

Ingredients:

- FOR THE FAJITAS
- ½ teaspoon ground cumin
- ½ teaspoon garlic powder
- ¼ teaspoon smoked paprika
- ¼ teaspoon onion powder
- ¼ teaspoon chili powder
- 1 pound boneless, skinless chicken breast, cut into ¼-inch strips
- 1 red bell pepper, cut into thin slices
- 1 green bell pepper, cut into thin slices
- 1 small red onion, cut into thin slices
- 2 tablespoons olive oil
- 8 (6-inch) tortillas
- OPTIONAL TOPPINGS
- Salsa
- Sour cream
- Pickled jalapeños
- Shredded lettuce

Directions:

1. Preheat the toaster oven to 375°F on AIR FRY for 5 minutes.
2. Place the air-fryer basket in the baking tray.
3. In a large bowl, stir the cumin, garlic powder, paprika, onion powder, and chili powder until well mixed. Add the chicken, bell peppers, onion, and oil, and toss to coat evenly.
4. Spread the chicken and veggies on the baking sheet.
5. In position 2, air fry for 15 minutes, tossing them halfway through, until cooked and the vegetables are lightly browned.
6. Serve tucked into the tortillas with your favorite toppings.

Air-fried Turkey Breast With Cherry Glaze

Servings: 6
Cooking Time: 54 Minutes

Ingredients:
- 1 (5-pound) turkey breast
- 2 teaspoons olive oil
- 1 teaspoon dried thyme
- ½ teaspoon dried sage
- 1 teaspoon salt
- ½ teaspoon freshly ground black pepper
- ½ cup cherry preserves
- 1 tablespoon chopped fresh thyme leaves
- 1 teaspoon soy sauce
- freshly ground black pepper

Directions:
1. All turkeys are built differently, so depending on the turkey breast and how your butcher has prepared it, you may need to trim the bottom of the ribs in order to get the turkey to sit upright in the air fryer oven without touching the heating element. The key to this recipe is getting the right size turkey breast. Once you've managed that, the rest is easy, so make sure your turkey breast fits into the air fryer oven before you Preheat the toaster oven oven.
2. Preheat the toaster oven to 350°F.
3. Brush the turkey breast all over with the olive oil. Combine the thyme, sage, salt and pepper and rub the outside of the turkey breast with the spice mixture.
4. Transfer the seasoned turkey breast to the air fryer oven, breast side up, and air-fry at 350°F for 25 minutes. Turn the turkey breast on its side and air-fry for another 12 minutes. Turn the turkey breast on the opposite side and air-fry for 12 more minutes. The internal temperature of the turkey breast should reach 165°F when fully cooked.
5. While the turkey is air-frying, make the glaze by combining the cherry preserves, fresh thyme, soy sauce and pepper in a small bowl. When the cooking time is up, return the turkey breast to an upright position and brush the glaze all over the turkey. Air-fry for a final 5 minutes, until the skin is nicely browned and crispy. Let the turkey rest, loosely tented with foil, for at least 5 minutes before slicing and serving.

Chicken Cutlets With Broccoli Rabe And Roasted Peppers

Servings: 2

Cooking Time: 10 Minutes

Ingredients:

- ½ bunch broccoli rabe
- olive oil, in a spray bottle
- salt and freshly ground black pepper
- ⅔ cup roasted red pepper strips
- 2 (4-ounce) boneless, skinless chicken breasts
- 2 tablespoons all-purpose flour
- 1 egg, beaten
- ⅓ cup seasoned breadcrumbs
- 2 slices aged provolone cheese

Directions:

1. Bring a medium saucepot of salted water to a boil on the stovetop. Blanch the broccoli rabe for 3 minutes in the boiling water and then drain. When it has cooled a little, squeeze out as much water as possible, drizzle a little olive oil on top, season with salt and black pepper and set aside. Dry the roasted red peppers with a clean kitchen towel and set them aside as well.

2. Place each chicken breast between 2 pieces of plastic wrap. Use a meat pounder to flatten the chicken breasts to about ½-inch thick. Season the chicken on both sides with salt and pepper.

3. Preheat the toaster oven to 400°F.

4. Set up a dredging station with three shallow dishes. Place the flour in one dish, the egg in a second dish and the breadcrumbs in a third dish. Coat the chicken on all sides with the flour. Shake off any excess flour and dip the chicken into the egg. Let the excess egg drip off and coat both sides of the chicken in the breadcrumbs. Spray the chicken with olive oil on both sides and transfer to the air fryer oven.

5. Air-fry the chicken at 400°F for 5 minutes. Turn the chicken over and air-fry for another minute. Then, top the chicken breast with the broccoli rabe and roasted peppers. Place a slice of the provolone cheese on top and secure it with a toothpick or two.

6. Air-fry at 360° for 3 to 4 minutes to melt the cheese and warm everything together.

Harissa Lemon Whole Chicken

Servings: 6

Cooking Time: 60 Minutes

Ingredients:

- 2 teaspoons kosher salt
- ½ teaspoon freshly ground black pepper
- ½ teaspoon ground cumin
- 2 garlic cloves
- 6 tablespoons harissa paste
- ½ lemon, juiced
- 1 whole lemon, zested
- 1 (5 pound) whole chicken

Directions:

1. Place salt, pepper, cumin, garlic cloves, harissa paste, lemon juice, and lemon zest in a food processor and pulse until they form a smooth puree.
2. Rub the puree all over the chicken, especially inside the cavity, and cover with plastic wrap.
3. Marinate for 1 hour at room temperature.
4. Preheat the toaster oven to 350°F.
5. Place the marinated chicken on the food tray, then insert the tray at low position in the preheated oven.
6. Select the Roast function, then press Start/Pause.
7. Remove when done, tent chicken with foil, and allow it to rest for 20 minutes before serving.

Chicken Wellington

Servings: 4

Cooking Time: 30 Minutes

Ingredients:

- 2 small (5- to 6-ounce) boneless, skinless chicken breast halves
- Kosher salt and freshly ground black pepper
- 2 teaspoons Italian seasoning
- 2 tablespoons olive oil
- 3 tablespoons unsalted butter, softened
- 3 ounces cream cheese, softened (about ⅓ cup)
- ¾ cup shredded Monterey Jack cheese
- ¼ cup grated Parmesan cheese
- 1 cup frozen (loose-pack) chopped spinach, thawed and squeezed dry
- ¾ cup chopped canned artichoke hearts, drained
- ½ teaspoon garlic powder
- 1 sheet frozen puff pastry, about 9 inches square, thawed (½ of a 17.3-ounce package)
- 1 large egg, lightly beaten

Directions:

1. Preheat the toaster oven to 425° F. Line a 12 x 12-inch baking pan with parchment paper.

2. Cut the chicken breasts in half lengthwise. Season each piece with the salt, pepper, and Italian seasoning. Fold the thinner end under the larger piece to make the chicken breasts into a rounded shape. Secure with toothpicks.

3. Heat a large skillet over medium-high heat. Add the olive oil and heat. Add the chicken breasts and brown well, turning to brown evenly. Remove from the skillet and set aside to cool. Remove the toothpicks.

4. Stir the butter, cream cheese, Monterey Jack, and Parmesan in a large bowl. Stir in the spinach, artichoke hearts, and garlic powder. Season with salt and pepper.

5. Roll out the puff pastry sheet on a lightly floured board until it makes a 12-inch square. Cut into four equal pieces. Spread one-fourth of the spinach-artichoke mixture on the surface of each pastry square to within ½ inch of all four edges. Place the chicken in the center of each. Gently fold the puff pastry up over the chicken and pinch the edges to seal tightly.

6. Place each chicken bundle, seam side down, on the prepared pan. Brush the top of each bundle lightly with the beaten egg. Bake for 25 to 30 minutes, or until the pastry is golden brown and crisp and a meat thermometer inserted into the chicken reaches 165°F.

Roast Chicken

Servings: 6
Cooking Time: 90 Minutes

Ingredients:
- Nonstick cooking spray
- 1 whole (3 ½ -pound) chicken
- Grated zest and juice of 1 lemon
- 1 tablespoon olive oil
- 1 ½ teaspoons kosher salt
- 1 teaspoon garlic powder
- ½ teaspoon dried thyme leaves
- ½ teaspoon freshly ground black pepper

Directions:
1. Preheat the toaster oven to 350°F. Spray a 12 x 12-inch baking pan with nonstick cooking spray.
2. Drizzle the chicken cavity with about half of the lemon juice. Place half of the juiced lemon into the chicken cavity. Truss the chicken using kitchen twine.
3. Rub the chicken evenly with the olive oil.
4. Stir the salt, garlic powder, lemon zest, thyme, and pepper in a small bowl. Using your fingertips, rub the seasonings evenly over the chicken. Place the chicken, breast side up, in the prepared pan. Drizzle with the remaining lemon juice.
5. Roast, uncovered, for 1 ¼ hours to 1 ½ hours, or until a meat thermometer registers 165°F. Let stand for 10 minutes before carving.

Thai Chicken Drumsticks

Servings: 4

Cooking Time: 20 Minutes

Ingredients:

- 2 tablespoons soy sauce
- ¼ cup rice wine vinegar
- 2 tablespoons chili garlic sauce
- 2 tablespoons sesame oil
- 1 teaspoon minced fresh ginger
- 2 teaspoons sugar
- ½ teaspoon ground coriander
- juice of 1 lime
- 8 chicken drumsticks (about 2½ pounds)
- ¼ cup chopped peanuts
- chopped fresh cilantro
- lime wedges

Directions:

1. Combine the soy sauce, rice wine vinegar, chili sauce, sesame oil, ginger, sugar, coriander and lime juice in a large bowl and mix together. Add the chicken drumsticks and marinate for 30 minutes.
2. Preheat the toaster oven to 370°F.
3. Place the chicken in the air fryer oven. It's ok if the ends of the drumsticks overlap a little. Spoon half of the marinade over the chicken, and reserve the other half.
4. Air-fry for 10 minutes. Turn the chicken over and pour the rest of the marinade over the chicken. Air-fry for an additional 10 minutes.
5. Transfer the chicken to a plate to rest and cool to an edible temperature. Pour the marinade from the bottom of the air fryer oven into a small saucepan and bring it to a simmer over medium-high heat. Simmer the liquid for 2 minutes so that it thickens enough to coat the back of a spoon.
6. Transfer the chicken to a serving platter, pour the sauce over the chicken and sprinkle the chopped peanuts on top. Garnish with chopped cilantro and lime wedges.

Foiled Rosemary Chicken Breasts

Servings: 2
Cooking Time: 30 Minutes

Ingredients:

- 2 skinless, boneless chicken breast halves
- Sauce:
- 3 tablespoons dry white wine
- 1 tablespoon Dijon mustard
- 2 tablespoons nonfat plain yogurt
- Salt and freshly ground black pepper to taste
- 2 rosemary sprigs

Directions:

1. Preheat the toaster oven to 400° F.
2. Place each breast on a 12 × 12-inch square of heavy-duty aluminum foil (or regular foil doubled) and turn up the edges of the foil.
3. Mix together the sauce ingredients and spoon over the chicken breasts. Lay a rosemary sprig on each breast. Bring up the edges of the foil and fold to form a sealed packet.
4. BAKE for 25 minutes or until juices run clear when the meat is pierced with a fork. Remove the rosemary sprigs.
5. BROIL for 5 minutes, or until lightly browned. Replace the sprigs and serve.

Crispy Chicken Parmesan

Servings: 4
Cooking Time: 12 Minutes

Ingredients:

- 4 skinless, boneless chicken breasts, pounded thin to ¼-inch thickness
- 1 teaspoon salt, divided
- ½ teaspoon black pepper, divided
- 1 cup flour
- 2 eggs
- 1 cup panko breadcrumbs
- ½ teaspoon dried oregano
- ½ cup grated Parmesan cheese

Directions:

1. Pat the chicken breasts with a paper towel. Season the chicken with ½ teaspoon of the salt and ¼ teaspoon of the pepper.
2. In a medium bowl, place the flour.
3. In a second bowl, whisk the eggs.
4. In a third bowl, place the breadcrumbs, oregano, cheese, and the remaining ½ teaspoon of salt and ¼ teaspoon of pepper.
5. Dredge the chicken in the flour and shake off the excess. Dip the chicken into the eggs and then into the breadcrumbs. Set the chicken on a plate and repeat with the remaining chicken pieces.
6. Preheat the toaster oven to 360°F.
7. Place the chicken in the air fryer oven and spray liberally with cooking spray. Air-fry for 8 minutes, turn the chicken breasts over, and cook another 4 minutes. When golden brown, check for an internal temperature of 165°F.

Chicken Breast With Chermoula Sauce

Servings: 4

Cooking Time: 15 Minutes

Ingredients:

- Chicken Ingredients
- 2 boneless skinless chicken breasts 1 tablespoon olive oil
- 1 teaspoon salt
- 1 teaspoon pepper
- Chermoula Ingredients
- 1 cup fresh cilantro
- 1 cup fresh parsley
- ¼ cup fresh mint
- ½ teaspoon red chili flakes
- ½ teaspoon cumin seeds
- ½ teaspoon coriander seeds
- 3 garlic cloves, peeled
- ½ cup extra virgin olive oil
- 1 lemon, zested and juiced
- ¾ teaspoons smoked paprika
- ¾ teaspoons salt

Directions:

1. Combine all the chermoula sauce ingredients in a blender or food processor. Pulse until smooth. Taste and add salt if needed. Place into a bowl and set aside.

2. Slice the chicken breast in half lengthwise and lightly pound with a meat tenderizer until both halves are about

3. ½-inch thick.

4. Preheat the toaster oven to 430°F.

5. Line the food tray with foil, then place the chicken breasts on the tray. Drizzle chicken with olive oil and season with salt and pepper.

6. Insert the food tray at top position in the preheated oven.

7. Select the Air Fry function, adjust time to 15 minutes, and press Start/Pause.

8. Remove when the chicken breast reaches an internal temperature of 160°F. Allow the chicken to rest for 5 minutes.

9. Brush the chermoula sauce over the chicken, or serve chicken with chermoula sauce on the side.

Sesame Chicken Breasts

Servings: 2
Cooking Time: 20 Minutes

Ingredients:
- Mixture:
- 2 tablespoons sesame oil
- 2 teaspoons soy sauce
- 2 teaspoons balsamic vinegar
- 2 skinless, boneless chicken breast filets
- 3 tablespoons sesame seeds

Directions:
1. Combine the mixture ingredients in a small bowl and brush the filets liberally. Reserve the mixture. Place the filets on a broiling rack with a pan underneath.
2. BROIL 15 minutes, or until the meat is tender and the juices, when the meat is pierced, run clear. Remove from the oven and brush the filets with the remaining mixture. Place the sesame seeds on a plate and press the chicken breast halves into the seeds, coating well.
3. BROIL for 5 minutes, or until the sesame seeds are browned.

Chicken Cordon Bleu

Servings: 4

Cooking Time: 25 Minutes

Ingredients:

- Oil spray (hand-pumped)
- 4 (4-ounce) chicken breasts
- 4 teaspoons Dijon mustard
- 4 slices Gruyère cheese
- 4 slices lean ham
- 1 cup all-purpose flour
- 2 large eggs
- 1 cup bread crumbs
- ½ cup Parmesan cheese

Directions:

1. Preheat the toaster oven to 350°F on AIR FRY for 5 minutes.
2. Place the air-fryer basket in the baking tray and generously spray it with the oil.
3. Place a chicken breast flat on a clean work surface and cut along the length of the breast, almost in half, holding the knife parallel to the counter. Open the breast up like a book and place it between two pieces of plastic wrap. Pound the chicken breast to about ¼-inch thick with a rolling pin or mallet. Repeat with the remaining breasts.
4. Spread the mustard on each breast, place a piece of cheese and ham in the center, and fold the sides of the breast over the cheese and ham. Roll the breast up from the unfolded sides to form a sealed packet. Secure with a toothpick.
5. Repeat with the remaining breasts.
6. Sprinkle the flour on a plate and set it on your work surface.
7. In a small bowl, whisk the eggs until well beaten and place next to the flour.
8. In a medium bowl, stir the bread crumbs and Parmesan and place next to the eggs.
9. Dredge the chicken rolls in the flour, then egg, then the bread crumb mixture, making sure they are completely breaded.
10. Arrange the chicken in the basket and spray lightly all over with the oil.
11. In position 2, air fry for 25 minutes, turning halfway through, until golden brown. Serve.

Buffalo Egg Rolls

Servings: 8

Cooking Time: 9 Minutes

Ingredients:

- 1 teaspoon water
- 1 tablespoon cornstarch
- 1 egg
- 2½ cups cooked chicken, diced or shredded (see opposite page)
- ⅓ cup chopped green onion
- ⅓ cup diced celery
- ⅓ cup buffalo wing sauce
- 8 egg roll wraps
- oil for misting or cooking spray
- Blue Cheese Dip
- 3 ounces cream cheese, softened
- ⅓ cup blue cheese, crumbled
- 1 teaspoon Worcestershire sauce
- ¼ teaspoon garlic powder
- ¼ cup buttermilk (or sour cream)

Directions:

1. Mix water and cornstarch in a small bowl until dissolved. Add egg, beat well, and set aside.
2. In a medium size bowl, mix together chicken, green onion, celery, and buffalo wing sauce.
3. Divide chicken mixture evenly among 8 egg roll wraps, spooning ½ inch from one edge.
4. Moisten all edges of each wrap with beaten egg wash.
5. Fold the short ends over filling, then roll up tightly and press to seal edges.
6. Brush outside of wraps with egg wash, then spritz with oil or cooking spray.
7. Place 4 egg rolls in air fryer oven.
8. Air-fry at 390°F for 9 minutes or until outside is brown and crispy.
9. While the rolls are cooking, prepare the Blue Cheese Dip. With a fork, mash together cream cheese and blue cheese.
10. Stir in remaining ingredients.
11. Dip should be just thick enough to slightly cling to egg rolls. If too thick, stir in buttermilk or milk 1 tablespoon at a time until you reach the desired consistency.
12. Cook remaining 4 egg rolls as in steps 7 and 8.
13. Serve while hot with Blue Cheese Dip, more buffalo wing sauce, or both.

Philly Chicken Cheesesteak Stromboli

Servings: 2

Cooking Time: 28 Minutes

Ingredients:

- ½ onion, sliced
- 1 teaspoon vegetable oil
- 2 boneless, skinless chicken breasts, partially frozen and sliced very thin on the bias (about 1 pound)
- 1 tablespoon Worcestershire sauce
- salt and freshly ground black pepper
- ½ recipe of Blue Jean Chef pizza dough, or 14 ounces of store-bought pizza dough
- 1½ cups grated Cheddar cheese
- ½ cup Cheese Whiz® (or other jarred cheese sauce), warmed gently in the microwave
- tomato ketchup for serving

Directions:

1. Preheat the toaster oven to 400°F.

2. Toss the sliced onion with oil and air-fry for 8 minutes, stirring halfway through the cooking time. Add the sliced chicken and Worcestershire sauce to the air fryer oven, and toss to evenly distribute the ingredients. Season the mixture with salt and freshly ground black pepper and air-fry for 8 minutes, stirring a couple of times during the cooking process. Remove the chicken and onion from the air fryer oven and let the mixture cool a little.

3. On a lightly floured surface, roll or press the pizza dough out into a 13-inch by 11-inch rectangle, with the long side closest to you. Sprinkle half of the Cheddar cheese over the dough leaving an empty 1-inch border from the edge farthest away from you. Top the cheese with the chicken and onion mixture, spreading it out evenly. Drizzle the cheese sauce over the meat and sprinkle the remaining Cheddar cheese on top.

4. Start rolling the stromboli away from you and toward the empty border. Make sure the filling stays tightly tucked inside the roll. Finally, tuck the ends of the dough in and pinch the seam shut. Place the seam side down and shape the Stromboli into a U-shape to fit in the air-fry oven. Cut 4 small slits with the tip of a sharp knife evenly in the top of the dough and lightly brush the stromboli with a little oil.

5. Preheat the toaster oven to 370°F.

6. Spray or brush the air fryer oven with oil and transfer the U-shaped stromboli to the air fryer oven. Air-fry for 12 minutes, turning the stromboli over halfway through the cooking time. (Use a plate to invert the stromboli out of the air fryer oven and then slide it back into the air fryer oven off the plate.)

7. To remove, carefully flip stromboli over onto a cutting board. Let it rest for a couple of minutes before serving. Slice the stromboli into 3-inch pieces and serve with ketchup for dipping, if desired.

Marinated Green Pepper And Pineapple Chicken

Servings: 4

Cooking Time: 20 Minutes

Ingredients:
- Marinade:
- 1 teaspoon finely chopped fresh ginger
- 2 garlic cloves, finely chopped
- 1 teaspoon toasted sesame oil
- 1 tablespoon brown sugar
- 2 tablespoons soy sauce
- ¾ cup dry white wine
- 2 skinless, boneless chicken breasts, cut into 1 × 3-inch strips
- 2 tablespoons chopped onion
- 1 bell pepper, chopped
- 1 5-ounce can pineapple chunks, drained
- 2 tablespoons grated unsweetened coconut

Directions:

1. Combine the marinade ingredients in a medium bowl and blend well. Add the chicken strips and spoon the mixture over them. Marinate in the refrigerator for at least 1 hour. Remove the strips from the marinade and place in an oiled or nonstick 8½ × 8½ × 2-inch square (cake) pan. Add the onion and pepper and mix well.

2. BROIL for 8 minutes. Then remove from the oven and, using tongs, turn the chicken, pepper, and onion pieces. (Spoon the reserved marinade over the pieces, if desired.)

3. BROIL again for 8 minutes, or until the chicken, pepper, and onion are cooked through and tender. Add the pineapple chunks and coconut and toss to mix well.

4. BROIL for another 4 minutes, or until the coconut is lightly browned.

Peanut Butter-barbeque Chicken

Servings: 4

Cooking Time: 20 Minutes

Ingredients:

- 1 pound boneless, skinless chicken thighs
- salt and pepper
- 1 large orange
- ½ cup barbeque sauce
- 2 tablespoons smooth peanut butter
- 2 tablespoons chopped peanuts for garnish (optional)
- cooking spray

Directions:

1. Season chicken with salt and pepper to taste. Place in a shallow dish or plastic bag.

2. Grate orange peel, squeeze orange and reserve 1 tablespoon of juice for the sauce.

3. Pour remaining juice over chicken and marinate for 30 minutes.

4. Mix together the reserved 1 tablespoon of orange juice, barbeque sauce, peanut butter, and 1 teaspoon grated orange peel.

5. Place ¼ cup of sauce mixture in a small bowl for basting. Set remaining sauce aside to serve with cooked chicken.

6. Preheat the toaster oven to 360°F. Spray air fryer oven with nonstick cooking spray.

7. Remove chicken from marinade, letting excess drip off. Place in air fryer oven and air-fry for 5 minutes. Turn chicken over and cook 5 minutes longer.

8. Brush both sides of chicken lightly with sauce.

9. Cook chicken 5 minutes, then turn thighs one more time, again brushing both sides lightly with sauce. Air-fry for 5 more minutes or until chicken is done and juices run clear.

10. Serve chicken with remaining sauce on the side and garnish with chopped peanuts if you like.

BEEF PORK AND LAMB

Smokehouse-style Beef Ribs

Servings: 3
Cooking Time: 25 Minutes

Ingredients:

- ¼ teaspoon Mild smoked paprika
- ¼ teaspoon Garlic powder
- ¼ teaspoon Onion powder
- ¼ teaspoon Table salt
- ¼ teaspoon Ground black pepper
- 3 10- to 12-ounce beef back ribs (not beef short ribs)

Directions:

1. Preheat the toaster oven to 350°F .
2. Mix the smoked paprika, garlic powder, onion powder, salt, and pepper in a small bowl until uniform. Massage and pat this mixture onto the ribs.
3. When the machine is at temperature, set the ribs in the air fryer oven in one layer, turning them on their sides if necessary, sort of like they're spooning but with at least ¼ inch air space between them. Air-fry for 25 minutes, turning once, until deep brown and sizzling.
4. Use kitchen tongs to transfer the ribs to a wire rack. Cool for 5 minutes before serving.

Traditional Pot Roast

Servings: 6
Cooking Time: 75 Minutes

Ingredients:

- 2 tablespoons olive oil
- 1 teaspoon garlic powder
- 1 teaspoon fresh thyme, chopped
- ¼ teaspoon sea salt
- ¼ teaspoon freshly ground black pepper
- 1 (3-pound) beef rump roast

Directions:

1. Preheat the toaster oven to 350°F on CONVECTION BAKE for 5 minutes.
2. In a small bowl, stir the oil, garlic, thyme, salt, and pepper. Spread the mixture all over the beef.
3. Place the air-fryer basket in the baking tray and place the beef in the basket.
4. In position 1, bake for 1 hour and 15 minutes until browned and the internal temperature reaches 145°F for medium.
5. Let the roast rest 10 minutes and serve.

Classic Pepperoni Pizza

Servings: 4

Cooking Time: 11 Minutes

Ingredients:

- Oil spray (hand-pumped)
- 1 pound premade pizza dough, or your favorite recipe
- ½ cup store-bought pizza sauce
- ¼ cup grated Parmesan cheese
- ¾ cup shredded mozzarella
- 10 to 12 slices pepperoni
- 2 tablespoons chopped fresh basil
- Pinch red pepper flakes

Directions:

1. Preheat the toaster oven to 425°F on BAKE for 5 minutes.
2. Spray the baking tray with the oil and spread the pizza dough with your fingertips so that it covers the tray. Prick the dough with a fork.
3. In position 2, bake for 8 minutes until the crust is lightly golden.
4. Take the crust out and spread with the pizza sauce, leaving a ½-inch border around the edge. Sprinkle with Parmesan and mozzarella cheeses and arrange the pepperoni on the pizza.
5. Bake for 3 minutes until the cheese is melted and bubbly.
6. Top with the basil and red pepper flakes and serve.

Beef And Spinach Braciole

Servings: 4
Cooking Time: 92 Minutes

Ingredients:

- 7-inch oven-safe baking pan or casserole
- ½ onion, finely chopped
- 1 teaspoon olive oil
- ⅓ cup red wine
- 2 cups crushed tomatoes
- 1 teaspoon Italian seasoning
- ½ teaspoon garlic powder
- ¼ teaspoon crushed red pepper flakes
- 2 tablespoons chopped fresh parsley
- 2 top round steaks (about 1½ pounds)
- salt and freshly ground black pepper
- 2 cups fresh spinach, chopped
- 1 clove minced garlic
- ½ cup roasted red peppers, julienned
- ½ cup grated pecorino cheese
- ¼ cup pine nuts, toasted and rough chopped
- 2 tablespoons olive oil

Directions:

1. Preheat the toaster oven to 400°F.

2. Toss the onions and olive oil together in a 7-inch metal baking pan or casserole dish. Air-fry at 400°F for 5 minutes, stirring a couple times during the cooking process. Add the red wine, crushed tomatoes, Italian seasoning, garlic powder, red pepper flakes and parsley and stir. Cover the pan tightly with aluminum foil, lower the air fryer oven temperature to 350°F and continue to air-fry for 15 minutes.

3. While the sauce is simmering, prepare the beef. Using a meat mallet, pound the beef until it is ¼-inch thick. Season both sides of the beef with salt and pepper. Combine the spinach, garlic, red peppers, pecorino cheese, pine nuts and olive oil in a medium bowl. Season with salt and freshly ground black pepper. Spread the mixture evenly over the steaks. Starting at one of the short ends, roll the beef around the filling, tucking in the sides as you roll to ensure the filling is completely enclosed. Secure the beef rolls with toothpicks.

4. Remove the baking pan with the sauce from the air fryer oven and set it aside. Preheat the toaster oven to 400°F.

5. Brush or spray the beef rolls with a little olive oil and air-fry at 400°F for 12 minutes, rotating the beef during the cooking process for even browning. When the beef is browned, submerge the rolls into the sauce in the baking pan, cover the pan with foil and return it to the air fryer oven. Air-fry at 250°F for 60 minutes.

6. Remove the beef rolls from the sauce. Cut each roll into slices and serve with pasta, ladling some of the sauce overtop.

Stuffed Bell Peppers

Servings: 4

Cooking Time: 10 Minutes

Ingredients:

- ¼ pound lean ground pork
- ¾ pound lean ground beef
- ¼ cup onion, minced
- 1 15-ounce can Red Gold crushed tomatoes
- 1 teaspoon Worcestershire sauce
- 1 teaspoon barbeque seasoning
- 1 teaspoon honey
- ½ teaspoon dried basil
- ½ cup cooked brown rice
- ½ teaspoon garlic powder
- ½ teaspoon oregano
- ½ teaspoon salt
- 2 small bell peppers

Directions:

1. Place pork, beef, and onion in air fryer oven baking pan and air-fry at 360°F for 5 minutes.
2. Stir to break apart chunks and cook 3 more minutes. Continue cooking and stirring in 2-minute intervals until meat is well done. Remove from pan and drain.
3. In a small saucepan, combine the tomatoes, Worcestershire, barbeque seasoning, honey, and basil. Stir well to mix in honey and seasonings.
4. In a large bowl, combine the cooked meat mixture, rice, garlic powder, oregano, and salt. Add ¼ cup of the seasoned crushed tomatoes. Stir until well mixed.
5. Cut peppers in half and remove stems and seeds.
6. Stuff each pepper half with one fourth of the meat mixture.
7. Place the peppers in air fryer oven and air-fry for 10 minutes, until peppers are crisp tender.
8. Heat remaining tomato sauce. Serve peppers with warm sauce spooned over top.

Crispy Smoked Pork Chops

Servings: 3

Cooking Time: 8 Minutes

Ingredients:

- ⅔ cup All-purpose flour or tapioca flour
- 1 Large egg white(s)
- 2 tablespoons Water
- 1½ cups Corn flake crumbs (gluten-free, if a concern)
- 3 ½-pound, ½-inch-thick bone-in smoked pork chops

Directions:

1. Preheat the toaster oven to 375°F.

2. Set up and fill three shallow soup plates or small pie plates on your counter: one for the flour; one for the egg white(s), whisked with the water until foamy; and one for the corn flake crumbs.

3. Set a chop in the flour and turn it several times, coating both sides and the edges. Gently shake off any excess flour, then set it in the beaten egg white mixture. Turn to coat both sides as well as the edges. Let any excess egg white slip back into the rest, then set the chop in the corn flake crumbs. Turn it several times, pressing gently to coat the chop evenly on both sides and around the edge. Set the chop aside and continue coating the remaining chop(s) in the same way.

4. Set the chops in the air fryer oven with as much air space between them as possible. Air-fry undisturbed for 8 minutes, or until the coating is crunchy and the chops are heated through.

5. Use kitchen tongs to transfer the chops to a wire rack and cool for a couple of minutes before serving.

Ribeye Steak With Blue Cheese Compound Butter

Servings: 2
Cooking Time: 12 Minutes

Ingredients:

- 5 tablespoons unsalted butter, softened
- ¼ cup crumbled blue cheese 2 teaspoons lemon juice
- 1 tablespoon freshly chopped chives
- Salt & freshly ground black pepper, to taste
- 2 (12 ounce) boneless ribeye steaks

Directions:

1. Mix together butter, blue cheese, lemon juice, and chives until smooth.
2. Season the butter to taste with salt and pepper.
3. Place the butter on plastic wrap and form into a 3-inch log, tying the ends of the plastic wrap together.
4. Place the butter in the fridge for 4 hours to harden.
5. Allow the steaks to sit at room temperature for 1 hour.
6. Pat the steaks dry with paper towels and season to taste with salt and pepper.
7. Insert the fry basket at top position in the Cosori Smart Air Fryer Toaster Oven.
8. Preheat the toaster Oven to 450°F.
9. Place the steaks in the fry basket in the preheated oven.
10. Select the Broil function, adjust time to 12 minutes, and press Start/Pause.
11. Remove when done and allow to rest for 5 minutes.
12. Remove the butter from the fridge, unwrap, and slice into ¾-inch pieces.
13. Serve the steak with one or two pieces of sliced compound butter.

Barbeque Ribs

Servings: 4
Cooking Time: 35 Minutes

Ingredients:

- 2 pounds pork spareribs or baby back ribs, silver skin removed
- 2 tablespoons brown sugar
- 1 teaspoon chili powder
- 1 teaspoon dry mustard
- Sea salt, for seasoning
- Freshly ground black pepper, for seasoning
- Oil spray (hand-pumped)
- 1 cup barbeque sauce

Directions:

1. Preheat the toaster oven to 375°F on AIR FRY for 5 minutes.
2. Cut the ribs into 4 bone sections or to fit in the basket.
3. In a small bowl, combine the brown sugar, chili powder, and mustard, and rub it all over the ribs.
4. Season the ribs with salt and pepper.
5. Place the air-fryer basket in the baking tray and spray it generously with the oil.
6. Arrange the ribs in the basket. There can be overlap if necessary.
7. In position 2, air fry for 35 minutes, turning halfway through, until the ribs are tender, browned, and crisp.
8. Baste the ribs with the barbeque sauce and serve.

Chipotle-glazed Meat Loaf

Servings: 4

Cooking Time: 65 Minutes

Ingredients:

- 1 ½ pounds lean ground beef
- ¼ cup finely chopped onion
- ½ cup crushed tortilla chips
- 1 teaspoon ground cumin
- ½ teaspoon chili powder
- ½ teaspoon garlic powder
- ½ teaspoon kosher salt
- ¼ teaspoon freshly ground black pepper
- 3 tablespoons chopped pickled jalapeños
- 3 tablespoons chunky salsa
- 1 large egg
- ⅓ cup ketchup
- 3 ½ teaspoons minced chipotle chilies in adobo sauce

Directions:

1. Preheat the toaster oven to 375 ºF. Line a 12 x 12-inch baking pan with aluminum foil.

2. Combine the ground beef, onion, tortilla chips, cumin, chili powder, garlic powder, salt, pepper, pickled jalapeños, salsa, and egg in a large bowl, stirring until blended well. Shape the meat mixture into a 9 x 5-inch loaf and place on the prepared pan.

3. Bake, uncovered, for 30 minutes. Carefully remove the meat loaf from the oven and spoon off any collected grease from the pan.

4. Place the ketchup in a small bowl and stir in the chipotle chilies in adobo sauce. Spread the ketchup mixture on top of the meat loaf. Continue to bake for an additional 25 to 35 minutes or until a meat thermometer registers 160 ºF. Let stand for 10 minutes before slicing.

Albóndigas

Servings: 4

Cooking Time: 15 Minutes

Ingredients:

- 1 pound Lean ground pork
- 3 tablespoons Very finely chopped trimmed scallions
- 3 tablespoons Finely chopped fresh cilantro leaves
- 3 tablespoons Plain panko bread crumbs (gluten-free, if a concern)
- 3 tablespoons Dry white wine, dry sherry, or unsweetened apple juice
- 1½ teaspoons Minced garlic
- 1¼ teaspoons Mild smoked paprika
- ¾ teaspoon Dried oregano
- ¾ teaspoon Table salt
- ¼ teaspoon Ground black pepper
- Olive oil spray

Directions:

1. Preheat the toaster oven to 400°F.

2. Mix the ground pork, scallions, cilantro, bread crumbs, wine or its substitute, garlic, smoked paprika, oregano, salt, and pepper in a bowl until the herbs and spices are evenly distributed in the mixture.

3. Lightly coat your clean hands with olive oil spray, then form the ground pork mixture into balls, using 2 tablespoons for each one. Spray your hands frequently so that the meat mixture doesn't stick.

4. Set the balls in the air fryer oven so that they're not touching, even if they're close together. Air-fry undisturbed for 15 minutes, or until well browned and an instant-read meat thermometer inserted into one or two balls registers 165°F.

5. Use a nonstick-safe spatula and kitchen tongs for balance to gently transfer the fragile balls to a wire rack to cool for 5 minutes before serving.

Zesty London Broil

Servings: 4

Cooking Time: 28 Minutes

Ingredients:

- ⅔ cup ketchup
- ¼ cup honey
- ¼ cup olive oil
- 2 tablespoons apple cider vinegar
- 2 tablespoons Worcestershire sauce
- 2 tablespoons minced onion
- ½ teaspoon paprika
- 1 teaspoon salt
- 1 teaspoon freshly ground black pepper
- 2 pounds London broil, top round or flank steak (about 1-inch thick)

Directions:

1. Combine the ketchup, honey, olive oil, apple cider vinegar, Worcestershire sauce, minced onion, paprika, salt and pepper in a small bowl and whisk together.

2. Generously pierce both sides of the meat with a fork or meat tenderizer and place it in a shallow dish. Pour the marinade mixture over the steak, making sure all sides of the meat get coated with the marinade. Cover and refrigerate overnight.

3. Preheat the toaster oven to 400°F.

4. Transfer the London broil to the air fryer oven and air-fry for 28 minutes, depending on how rare or well done you like your steak. Flip the steak over halfway through the cooking time.

5. Remove the London broil from the air fryer oven and let it rest for five minutes on a cutting board. To serve, thinly slice the meat against the grain and transfer to a serving platter.

Pork Taco Gorditas

Servings: 4

Cooking Time: 21 Minutes

Ingredients:

- 1 pound lean ground pork
- 2 tablespoons chili powder
- 2 tablespoons ground cumin
- 1 teaspoon dried oregano
- 2 teaspoons paprika
- 1 teaspoon garlic powder
- ½ cup water
- 1 (15-ounce) can pinto beans, drained and rinsed
- ½ cup taco sauce
- salt and freshly ground black pepper
- 2 cups grated Cheddar cheese
- 5 (12-inch) flour tortillas
- 4 (8-inch) crispy corn tortilla shells
- 4 cups shredded lettuce
- 1 tomato, diced
- ⅓ cup sliced black olives
- sour cream, for serving
- tomato salsa, for serving

Directions:

1. Preheat the toaster oven to 400°F.

2. Place the ground pork in the air fryer oven and air-fry at 400°F for 10 minutes, stirring a few times during the cooking process to gently break up the meat. Combine the chili powder, cumin, oregano, paprika, garlic powder and water in a small bowl. Stir the spice mixture into the browned pork. Stir in the beans and taco sauce and air-fry for an additional minute. Transfer the pork mixture to a bowl. Season to taste with salt and freshly ground black pepper.

3. Sprinkle ½ cup of the shredded cheese in the center of four of the flour tortillas, making sure to leave a 2-inch border around the edge free of cheese and filling. Divide the pork mixture among the four tortillas, placing it on top of the cheese. Place a crunchy corn tortilla on top of the pork and top with shredded lettuce, diced tomatoes, and black olives. Cut the remaining flour tortilla into 4 quarters. These quarters of tortilla will serve as the bottom of the gordita. Place one quarter tortilla on top of each gordita and fold the edges of the bottom flour tortilla up over the sides, enclosing the filling. While holding the seams down, brush the bottom of the gordita with olive oil and place the seam side down on the countertop while you finish the remaining three gorditas.

4. Preheat the toaster oven to 380°F.

5. Air-fry one gordita at a time. Transfer the gordita carefully to the air fryer oven, seam side down. Brush or spray the top tortilla with oil and air-fry for 5 minutes. Carefully turn the gordita over and air-fry for an additional 5 minutes, until both sides are browned. When finished air frying all four gorditas, layer them back into the air fryer oven for an additional minute to make sure they are all warm before serving with sour cream and salsa.

Lime-ginger Pork Tenderloin

Servings: 4

Cooking Time: 26 Minutes

Ingredients:

- ½ cup packed dark brown sugar
- Juice of ½ lime
- 2 teaspoons fresh ginger, peeled and grated
- 1 teaspoon minced garlic
- 2 (1-pound) extra-lean pork tenderloins, trimmed of fat
- Sea salt, for seasoning
- Freshly ground black pepper, for seasoning
- 1 tablespoon olive oil

Directions:

1. Preheat the toaster oven to 400°F on CONVECTION BAKE for 5 minutes.
2. In a small bowl, stir the sugar, lime juice, ginger, and garlic together.
3. Lightly season the pork tenderloins all over with salt and pepper.
4. Heat the oil in a large skillet over medium-high heat. Brown the pork on all sides, about 6 minutes in total.
5. Place the air-fryer basket in the baking tray and place the tenderloins in the basket.
6. Brush the pork all over with the ginger-lime mixture.
7. In position 2, bake for 20 minutes, basting the pork at 10 minutes, until it reaches an internal temperature of about 145°F.
8. Let the pork rest for 10 minutes and serve.

Beef Al Carbon (street Taco Meat)

Servings: 6

Cooking Time: 8 Minutes

Ingredients:

- 1½ pounds sirloin steak, cut into ½-inch cubes
- ¾ cup lime juice
- ½ cup extra-virgin olive oil
- 1 teaspoon ground cumin
- 2 teaspoons garlic powder
- 1 teaspoon salt

Directions:

1. In a large bowl, toss together the steak, lime juice, olive oil, cumin, garlic powder, and salt. Allow the meat to marinate for 30 minutes. Drain off all the marinade and pat the meat dry with paper towels.
2. Preheat the toaster oven to 400°F.
3. Place the meat in the air fryer oven and spray with cooking spray. Cook the meat for 5 minutes, toss the meat, and continue cooking another 3 minutes, until slightly crispy.

Pesto Pork Chops

Servings: 2

Cooking Time: 15 Minutes

Ingredients:

- 2 (6-ounce) boneless pork loin chops
- 2 tablespoons basil pesto

Directions:

1. Preheat the toaster oven to 375°F on AIR FRY for 5 minutes.

2. Rub the pork chops all over with the pesto and set aside for 15 minutes.

3. Place the air-fryer basket in the baking tray and arrange the pork in the basket with no overlap.

4. In position 2, air fry for 15 minutes, turning halfway through, until the chops are lightly browned and have an internal temperature of 145°F.

5. Let the meat rest for 10 minutes and serve.

Minted Lamb Chops

Servings: 4

Cooking Time: 15 Minutes

Ingredients:

- Mint mixture:
- 4 tablespoons finely chopped fresh mint
- 2 tablespoons nonfat yogurt
- 1 tablespoon olive oil
- Salt and freshly ground black pepper to taste
- 4 lean lamb chops, fat trimmed, approximately ¾ inch thick
- 1 tablespoon balsamic vinegar

Directions:

1. Combine the mint mixture ingredients in a small bowl, stirring well to blend. Set aside. Place the lamp chops on a broiling rack with a pan underneath.

2. BROIL the lamb chops for 10 minutes, or until they are slightly pink. Remove from the oven and brush one side liberally with balsamic vinegar. Turn the chops over with tongs and spread with the mint mixture, using all of the mixture.

3. BROIL again for 5 minutes, or until lightly browned.

Pork Loin

Servings: 8

Cooking Time: 50 Minutes

Ingredients:

- 1 tablespoon lime juice
- 1 tablespoon orange marmalade
- 1 teaspoon coarse brown mustard
- 1 teaspoon curry powder
- 1 teaspoon dried lemongrass
- 2-pound boneless pork loin roast
- salt and pepper
- cooking spray

Directions:

1. Mix together the lime juice, marmalade, mustard, curry powder, and lemongrass.
2. Rub mixture all over the surface of the pork loin. Season to taste with salt and pepper.
3. Spray air fryer oven with nonstick spray and place pork roast diagonally in the pan.
4. Air-fry at 360°F for approximately 50 minutes, until roast registers 130°F on a meat thermometer.
5. Wrap roast in foil and let rest for 10minutes before slicing.

Pretzel-coated Pork Tenderloin

Servings: 4

Cooking Time: 10 Minutes

Ingredients:

- 1 Large egg white(s)
- 2 teaspoons Dijon mustard (gluten-free, if a concern)
- 1½ cups (about 6 ounces) Crushed pretzel crumbs
- 1 pound (4 sections) Pork tenderloin, cut into ¼-pound (4-ounce) sections
- Vegetable oil spray

Directions:

1. Preheat the toaster oven to 350°F .
2. Set up and fill two shallow soup plates or small pie plates on your counter: one for the egg white(s), whisked with the mustard until foamy; and one for the pretzel crumbs.
3. Dip a section of pork tenderloin in the egg white mixture and turn it to coat well, even on the ends. Let any excess egg white mixture slip back into the rest, then set the pork in the pretzel crumbs. Roll it several times, pressing gently, until the pork is evenly coated, even on the ends. Generously coat the pork section with vegetable oil spray, set it aside, and continue coating and spraying the remaining sections.
4. Set the pork sections in the air fryer oven with at least ¼ inch between them. Air-fry undisturbed for 10 minutes, or until an instant-read meat thermometer inserted into the center of one section registers 145°F.
5. Use kitchen tongs to transfer the pieces to a wire rack. Cool for 3 to 5 minutes before serving.

Better-than-chinese-take-out Pork Ribs

Servings: 3

Cooking Time: 35 Minutes

Ingredients:

- 1½ tablespoons Hoisin sauce (gluten-free, if a concern)
- 1½ tablespoons Regular or low-sodium soy sauce or gluten-free tamari sauce
- 1½ tablespoons Shaoxing (Chinese cooking rice wine), dry sherry, or white grape juice
- 1½ teaspoons Minced garlic
- ¾ teaspoon Ground dried ginger
- ¾ teaspoon Ground white pepper
- 1½ pounds Pork baby back rib rack(s), cut into 2-bone pieces

Directions:

1. Mix the hoisin sauce, soy or tamari sauce, Shaoxing or its substitute, garlic, ginger, and white pepper in a large bowl. Add the rib sections and stir well to coat. Cover and refrigerate for at least 2 hours or up to 24 hours, stirring the rib sections in the marinade occasionally.

2. Preheat the toaster oven to 350°F . Set the ribs in their bowl on the counter as the machine heats.

3. When the machine is at temperature, set the rib pieces on their sides in a single layer in the air fryer oven with as much air space between them as possible. Air-fry for 35 minutes, turning and rearranging the pieces once, until deeply browned and sizzling.

4. Use kitchen tongs to transfer the rib pieces to a large serving bowl or platter. Wait a minute or two before serving them so the meat can reabsorb some of its own juices.

VEGETABLES AND VEGETARIAN

Parmesan Asparagus

Servings: 2
Cooking Time: 5 Minutes

Ingredients:

- 1 bunch asparagus, stems trimmed
- 1 teaspoon olive oil
- salt and freshly ground black pepper
- ¼ cup coarsely grated Parmesan cheese
- ½ lemon

Directions:

1. Preheat the toaster oven to 400°F.
2. Toss the asparagus with the oil and season with salt and freshly ground black pepper.
3. Transfer the asparagus to the air fryer oven and air-fry at 400°F for 5 minutes, turn the asparagus once or twice during the cooking process.
4. When the asparagus is cooked to your liking, sprinkle the asparagus generously with the Parmesan cheese and close the air fryer oven again. Let the asparagus sit for 1 minute in the turned-off air fryer oven. Then, remove the asparagus, transfer it to a serving dish and finish with a grind of black pepper and a squeeze of lemon juice.

Onions

Servings: 4
Cooking Time: 18 Minutes

Ingredients:

- 2 yellow onions (Vidalia or 1015 recommended)
- salt and pepper
- ¼ teaspoon ground thyme
- ¼ teaspoon smoked paprika
- 2 teaspoons olive oil
- 1 ounce Gruyère cheese, grated

Directions:

1. Peel onions and halve lengthwise (vertically).
2. Sprinkle cut sides of onions with salt, pepper, thyme, and paprika.
3. Place each onion half, cut-surface up, on a large square of aluminum foil. Pull sides of foil up to cup around onion. Drizzle cut surface of onions with oil.
4. Crimp foil at top to seal closed.
5. Place wrapped onions in air fryer oven and air-fry at 390°F for 18 minutes. When done, onions should be soft enough to pierce with fork but still slightly firm.
6. Open foil just enough to sprinkle each onion with grated cheese.
7. Air-fry for 30 seconds to 1 minute to melt cheese.

Lentil-stuffed Zucchini

Servings: 2

Cooking Time: 50 Minutes

Ingredients:

- 2 large zucchini
- 2 teaspoons olive oil
- 1 (15-ounce) can low-sodium lentils, drained and rinsed
- 1 large tomato, chopped
- 1 scallion, both white and green parts, chopped
- ½ jalapeño pepper, minced
- ½ cup corn kernels, fresh or frozen (thawed)
- 1 tablespoon fresh cilantro, chopped
- 1 teaspoon minced garlic
- 1 teaspoon ground cumin
- ¼ teaspoon chili powder
- ½ cup shredded Monterey Jack cheese

Directions:

1. Preheat the toaster oven to 400°F on BAKE for 5 minutes.
2. Line the baking tray with parchment paper.
3. Cut the zucchini in half lengthwise and scoop out the insides so that you have a hollow shell (about ¼-inch thick all the way around).
4. Lightly oil both sides of the zucchini shells and set them on the baking sheet.
5. In a large bowl, stir the lentils, tomato, scallion, jalapeño, corn, cilantro, garlic, cumin, and chili powder until well mixed.
6. Spoon the lentil mixture into the zucchini and top with the cheese.
7. Bake for 50 minutes. The zucchini should be tender, the filling heated through, and the cheese melted and lightly browned. Serve.

Broiled Tomatoes

Servings: 4

Cooking Time: 10 Minutes

Ingredients:

- 2 medium tomatoes
- Filling:
- 2 tablespoons grated Parmesan cheese
- 2 tablespoons bread crumbs
- 2 tablespoons olive oil
- 1 teaspoon dried oregano or 1 tablespoon chopped fresh oregano
- 1 teaspoon garlic powder or 2 garlic cloves, minced
- Salt and freshly ground black pepper to taste

Directions:

1. Slice the tomatoes in half through the stem scar (top) and carefully scoop out the seeds and flesh with a teaspoon. (Remove and discard about 1 tablespoon each.)

2. Mix together the filling ingredients in a small bowl and adjust the seasonings. Fill each tomato half cavity with equal portions of the mixture. Place the tomato halves in an oiled or nonstick 8½ × 8½ × 2-inch square baking (cake) pan.

3. BROIL for 10 minutes, or until the tomatoes are cooked and the tops are browned.

Crisp Cajun Potato Wedges

Servings: 2

Cooking Time: 70 Minutes

Ingredients:

- 2 medium baking potatoes, scrubbed, halved, and cut lengthwise into ½-inch-wide wedges
- 1 tablespoon vegetable oil
- Cajun seasonings:
- ¼ teaspoon chili powder
- ⅛ teaspoon cayenne
- ⅛ teaspoon dry mustard
- ⅛ teaspoon salt
- ⅛ teaspoon cumin
- ¼ teaspoon onion powder
- ¼ teaspoon paprika

Directions:

1. Preheat the toaster oven to 450° F.

2. Soak the potato wedges in cold water for 10 minutes to crisp. Drain on paper towels. Brush with the oil.

3. Combine the Cajun seasonings in a small bowl, add the wedges, and toss to coat well. Transfer to an oiled or nonstick 8½ × 8½ × 2-inch square baking (cake) pan.

4. BAKE, covered, for 40 minutes, or until the potatoes are tender. Carefully remove the cover.

5. BROIL for 20 minutes to crisp, turning with a tongs every 5 minutes until the desired crispness is achieved.

Five-spice Roasted Sweet Potatoes

Servings: 4

Cooking Time: 12 Minutes

Ingredients:

- ½ teaspoon ground cinnamon
- ¼ teaspoon ground cumin
- ¼ teaspoon paprika
- 1 teaspoon chile powder
- ⅛ teaspoon turmeric
- ½ teaspoon salt (optional)
- freshly ground black pepper
- 2 large sweet potatoes, peeled and cut into ¾-inch cubes (about 3 cups)
- 1 tablespoon olive oil

Directions:

1. In a large bowl, mix together cinnamon, cumin, paprika, chile powder, turmeric, salt, and pepper to taste.
2. Add potatoes and stir well.
3. Drizzle the seasoned potatoes with the olive oil and stir until evenly coated.
4. Place seasoned potatoes in the air fryer oven baking pan or an ovenproof dish that fits inside your air fryer oven.
5. Air-fry for 6 minutes at 390°F, stop, and stir well.
6. Air-fry for an additional 6 minutes.

Mushrooms, Sautéed

Servings: 4

Cooking Time: 4 Minutes

Ingredients:

- 8 ounces sliced white mushrooms, rinsed and well drained
- ¼ teaspoon garlic powder
- 1 tablespoon Worcestershire sauce

Directions:

1. Place mushrooms in a large bowl and sprinkle with garlic powder and Worcestershire. Stir well to distribute seasonings evenly.
2. Place in air fryer oven and air-fry at 390°F for 4 minutes, until tender.

Yellow Squash

Servings: 4

Cooking Time: 10 Minutes

Ingredients:

- 1 large yellow squash (about 1½ cups)
- 2 eggs
- ¼ cup buttermilk
- 1 cup panko breadcrumbs
- ¼ cup white cornmeal
- ½ teaspoon salt
- oil for misting or cooking spray

Directions:

1. Preheat the toaster oven to 390°F.
2. Cut the squash into ¼-inch slices.
3. In a shallow dish, beat together eggs and buttermilk.
4. In sealable plastic bag or container with lid, combine ¼ cup panko crumbs, white cornmeal, and salt. Shake to mix well.
5. Place the remaining ¾ cup panko crumbs in a separate shallow dish.
6. Dump all the squash slices into the egg/buttermilk mixture. Stir to coat.
7. Remove squash from buttermilk mixture with a slotted spoon, letting excess drip off, and transfer to the panko/cornmeal mixture. Close bag or container and shake well to coat.
8. Remove squash from crumb mixture, letting excess fall off. Return squash to egg/buttermilk mixture, stirring gently to coat. If you need more liquid to coat all the squash, add a little more buttermilk.
9. Remove each squash slice from egg wash and dip in a dish of ¾ cup panko crumbs.
10. Mist squash slices with oil or cooking spray and place in air fryer oven. Squash should be in a single layer, but it's okay if the slices crowd together and overlap a little.
11. Air-fry at 390°F for 5 minutes. Break up any that have stuck together. Mist again with oil or spray.
12. Cook 5 minutes longer and check. If necessary, mist again with oil and cook an additional two minutes, until squash slices are golden brown and crisp.

Glazed Carrots

Servings: 4

Cooking Time: 10 Minutes

Ingredients:

- 2 teaspoons honey
- 1 teaspoon orange juice
- ½ teaspoon grated orange rind
- ⅛ teaspoon ginger
- 1 pound baby carrots
- 2 teaspoons olive oil
- ¼ teaspoon salt

Directions:

1. Combine honey, orange juice, grated rind, and ginger in a small bowl and set aside.
2. Toss the carrots, oil, and salt together to coat well and pour them into the air fryer oven.
3. Air-fry at 390°F for 5 minutes. Stir a little and air-fry for 4 minutes more, until carrots are barely tender.
4. Pour carrots into air fryer oven baking pan.
5. Stir the honey mixture to combine well, pour glaze over carrots, and stir to coat.
6. Air-fry at 360°F for 1 minute or just until heated through.

Ratatouille

Servings: 4

Cooking Time: 60 Minutes

Ingredients:

- Oil spray (hand-pumped)
- 1 eggplant, peeled and diced into ½-inch chunks
- 2 tomatoes, diced
- 1 zucchini, diced
- 2 bell peppers (any color), diced
- ½ red onion, chopped
- ½ cup tomato paste
- 2 teaspoons minced garlic
- 1 teaspoon dried basil
- ¼ teaspoon sea salt
- ⅛ teaspoon freshly ground black pepper
- Pinch red pepper flakes
- ½ cup low-sodium vegetable broth

Directions:

1. Place the rack in position 1 and preheat oven to 350°F on CONVECTION BAKE for 5 minutes.
2. Lightly coat a 1½-quart casserole dish with oil spray.
3. In a large bowl, toss the eggplant, tomatoes, zucchini, bell peppers, onion, tomato paste, garlic, basil, salt, black pepper, and red pepper flakes until well combined.
4. Transfer the vegetable mixture to the casserole dish, pour in the vegetable broth, and cover tightly with foil or a lid.
5. Convection bake for 1 hour, stirring once at the halfway mark, until the vegetables are very tender. Serve.

Blistered Tomatoes

Servings: 20
Cooking Time: 15 Minutes

Ingredients:

- 1½ pounds Cherry or grape tomatoes
- Olive oil spray
- 1½ teaspoons Balsamic vinegar
- ¼ teaspoon Table salt
- ¼ teaspoon Ground black pepper

Directions:

1. Put the pan in a drawer-style air fryer oven, or a baking tray in the lower third of a toaster oven–style air fryer oven. Place a 6-inch round cake pan in the pan or on the tray for a small batch, a 7-inch round cake pan for a medium batch, or an 8-inch round cake pan for a large one. Heat the air fryer oven to 400°F with the pan in the air fryer oven. When the machine is at temperature, keep heating the pan for 5 minutes more.

2. Place the tomatoes in a large bowl, coat them with the olive oil spray, toss gently, then spritz a couple of times more, tossing after each spritz, until the tomatoes are glistening.

3. Pour the tomatoes into the cake pan and air-fry undisturbed for 10 minutes, or until they split and begin to brown.

4. Use kitchen tongs and a nonstick-safe spatula, or silicone baking mitts, to remove the cake pan from the air fryer oven. Toss the hot tomatoes with the vinegar, salt, and pepper. Cool in the pan for a few minutes before serving.

Tasty Golden Potatoes

Servings: 4
Cooking Time: 38 Minutes

Ingredients:

- 2 cups peeled and shredded potatoes
- ½ cup peeled and shredded carrots
- ¼ cup shredded onion
- 1 teaspoon salt
- 1 teaspoon dried rosemary
- 1 teaspoon dried cumin
- 3 tablespoons vegetable oil
- Salt and freshly ground black pepper to taste

Directions:

1. Preheat the toaster oven to 400° F.

2. Mix all the ingredients together in a 1-quart 8½ × 8½ × 2-inch ovenproof baking dish. Adjust the seasonings to taste. Cover the dish with aluminum foil.

3. BAKE, covered, for 30 minutes, or until tender. Remove the cover.

4. BROIL for 8 minutes, or until the top is browned.

Brown Rice And Goat Cheese Croquettes

Servings: 3

Cooking Time: 8 Minutes

Ingredients:

- ¾ cup Water
- 6 tablespoons Raw medium-grain brown rice, such as brown Arborio
- ½ cup Shredded carrot
- ¼ cup Walnut pieces
- 3 tablespoons (about 1½ ounces) Soft goat cheese
- 1 tablespoon Pasteurized egg substitute, such as Egg Beaters (gluten-free, if a concern)
- ¼ teaspoon Dried thyme
- ¼ teaspoon Table salt
- ¼ teaspoon Ground black pepper
- Olive oil spray

Directions:

1. Combine the water, rice, and carrots in a small saucepan set over medium-high heat. Bring to a boil, stirring occasionally. Cover, reduce the heat to very low, and simmer very slowly for 45 minutes, or until the water has been absorbed and the rice is tender. Set aside, covered, for 10 minutes.

2. Scrape the contents of the saucepan into a food processor. Cool for 10 minutes.

3. Preheat the toaster oven to 400°F.

4. Put the nuts, cheese, egg substitute, thyme, salt, and pepper into the food processor. Cover and pulse to a coarse paste, stopping the machine at least once to scrape down the inside of the canister.

5. Uncover the food processor; scrape down and remove the blade. Using wet, clean hands, form the mixture into two 4-inch-diameter patties for a small batch, three 4-inch-diameter patties for a medium batch, or four 4-inch-diameter patties for a large one. Generously coat both sides of the patties with olive oil spray.

6. Set the patties in the air fryer oven with as much air space between them as possible. Air-fry undisturbed for 8 minutes, or until brown and crisp.

7. Use a nonstick-safe spatula to transfer the croquettes to a wire rack. Cool for 5 minutes before serving.

Buttery Rolls

Servings: 6

Cooking Time: 14 Minutes

Ingredients:

- 6½ tablespoons Room-temperature whole or low-fat milk
- 3 tablespoons plus 1 teaspoon Butter, melted and cooled
- 3 tablespoons plus 1 teaspoon (or 1 medium egg, well beaten) Pasteurized egg substitute, such as Egg Beaters
- 1½ tablespoons Granulated white sugar
- 1¼ teaspoons Instant yeast
- ¼ teaspoon Table salt
- 2 cups, plus more for dusting All-purpose flour
- Vegetable oil
- Additional melted butter, for brushing

Directions:

1. Stir the milk, melted butter, pasteurized egg substitute (or whole egg), sugar, yeast, and salt in a medium bowl to combine. Stir in the flour just until the mixture makes a soft dough.

2. Lightly flour a clean, dry work surface. Turn the dough out onto the work surface. Knead the dough for 5 minutes to develop the gluten.

3. Lightly oil the inside of a clean medium bowl. Gather the dough into a compact ball and set it in the bowl. Turn the dough over so that its surface has oil on it all over. Cover the bowl tightly with plastic wrap and set aside in a warm, draft-free place until the dough has doubled in bulk, about 1½ hours.

4. Punch down the dough, then turn it out onto a clean, dry work surface. Divide it into 5 even balls for a small batch, 6 balls for a medium batch, or 8 balls for a large one.

5. For a small batch, lightly oil the inside of a 6-inch round cake pan and set the balls around its perimeter, separating them as much as possible.

6. For a medium batch, lightly oil the inside of a 7-inch round cake pan and set the balls in it with one ball at its center, separating them as much as possible.

7. For a large batch, lightly oil the inside of an 8-inch round cake pan and set the balls in it with one at the center, separating them as much as possible.

8. Cover with plastic wrap and set aside to rise for 30 minutes.

9. Preheat the toaster oven to 350°F .

10. Uncover the pan and brush the rolls with a little melted butter, perhaps ½ teaspoon per roll. When the machine is at temperature, set the cake pan in the air fryer oven. Air-fry undisturbed for 14 minutes, or until the rolls have risen and browned.

11. Using kitchen tongs and a nonstick-safe spatula, two hot pads, or silicone baking mitts, transfer the cake pan from the air fryer oven to a wire rack. Cool the rolls in the pan for a minute or two. Turn the rolls out onto a wire rack, set them top side up again, and cool for at least another couple of minutes before serving warm.

Roasted Vegetables

Servings: 4

Cooking Time: 20 Minutes

Ingredients:

- 1 1-pound package frozen vegetable mixture
- 1 tablespoon olive oil
- 1 tablespoon bread crumbs
- 1 teaspoon dried oregano
- 1 teaspoon ground cumin
- Salt and freshly ground black pepper to taste
- 1 tablespoon grated Parmesan cheese
- 1 tablespoon chopped walnuts

Directions:

1. Blend all the ingredients in an oiled or nonstick 8½ × 8½ × 2-inch square baking (cake) pan, tossing to coat the vegetable pieces with the oil, bread crumbs, and seasonings. Adjust the seasonings.

2. BROIL for 10 minutes. Remove the pan from the oven and turn the pieces with tongs. Add the cheese and walnuts. Broil for another 10 minutes, or until the vegetables are lightly browned. Adjust the seasonings and serve.

Marjoram New Potatoes

Servings: 2

Cooking Time: 40 Minutes

Ingredients:

- 6 small new red potatoes, scrubbed and halved
- 1 tablespoon olive oil
- 1 tablespoon balsamic vinegar
- 1 tablespoon fresh marjoram leaves, chopped, or 1 teaspoon dried marjoram
- Salt and freshly ground black pepper to taste

Directions:

1. Preheat the toaster oven to 400° F.

2. Combine all the ingredients in a medium bowl and mix well to coat the potatoes.

3. Place in an oiled or nonstick 8½ × 8½ × 2-inch square baking (cake) pan.

4. BAKE, covered, for 30 minutes, or until the potatoes are tender.

5. BROIL 10 minutes to brown to your preference. Serve with balsamic vinegar in a small pitcher to drizzle over.

Mashed Potato Tots

Servings: 18
Cooking Time: 10 Minutes

Ingredients:
- 1 medium potato or 1 cup cooked mashed potatoes
- 1 tablespoon real bacon bits
- 2 tablespoons chopped green onions, tops only
- ¼ teaspoon onion powder
- 1 teaspoon dried chopped chives
- salt
- 2 tablespoons flour
- 1 egg white, beaten
- ½ cup panko breadcrumbs
- oil for misting or cooking spray

Directions:
1. If using cooked mashed potatoes, jump to step 4.
2. Peel potato and cut into ½-inch cubes. (Small pieces cook more quickly.) Place in saucepan, add water to cover, and heat to boil. Lower heat slightly and continue cooking just until tender, about 10 minutes.
3. Drain potatoes and place in ice cold water. Allow to cool for a minute or two, then drain well and mash.
4. Preheat the toaster oven to 390°F.
5. In a large bowl, mix together the potatoes, bacon bits, onions, onion powder, chives, salt to taste, and flour. Add egg white and stir well.
6. Place panko crumbs on a sheet of wax paper.
7. For each tot, use about 2 teaspoons of potato mixture. To shape, drop the measure of potato mixture onto panko crumbs and push crumbs up and around potatoes to coat edges. Then turn tot over to coat other side with crumbs.
8. Mist tots with oil or cooking spray and place in air fryer oven, crowded but not stacked.
9. Air-fry at 390°F for 10 minutes, until browned and crispy.
10. Repeat steps 8 and 9 to cook remaining tots.

Vegetable–goat Cheese Flatbreads

Servings: 4

Cooking Time: 17 Minutes

Ingredients:

- 1 (8-inch-wide) rectangular flatbread
- ½ cup store-bought sun-dried tomato pesto
- 12 thin zucchini slices
- ¼ cup mushrooms, thinly sliced
- ¼ red onion, thinly sliced
- 1 tomato, chopped
- ¾ cup goat cheese, crumbled

Directions:

1. Line the baking tray with parchment paper. Place the flatbread on the baking tray and TOAST in position 2 for 5 minutes on medium darkness until lightly crisped. Remove from the oven.

2. Preheat the toaster oven to 400°F on BAKE.

3. Spread the pesto on the flatbread, leaving a ½-inch border along the edge. Scatter the zucchini, mushrooms, onion, and tomato evenly on the flatbread. Top with the goat cheese.

4. Place the baking tray in position 2 and bake for 10 to 12 minutes until crispy and the cheese is melted and lightly browned. Serve.

Fried Green Tomatoes With Sriracha Mayo

Servings: 4

Cooking Time: 12 Minutes

Ingredients:

- 3 green tomatoes
- salt and freshly ground black pepper
- ⅓ cup all-purpose flour
- 2 eggs
- ½ cup buttermilk
- 1 cup panko breadcrumbs
- 1 cup cornmeal
- olive oil, in a spray bottle
- fresh thyme sprigs or chopped fresh chives
- Sriracha Mayo
- ½ cup mayonnaise
- 1 to 2 tablespoons sriracha hot sauce
- 1 tablespoon milk

Directions:

1. Cut the tomatoes in ¼-inch slices. Pat them dry with a clean kitchen towel and season generously with salt and pepper.

2. Set up a dredging station using three shallow dishes. Place the flour in the first shallow dish, whisk the eggs and buttermilk together in the second dish, and combine the panko breadcrumbs and cornmeal in the third dish.

3. Preheat the toaster oven to 400°F.

4. Dredge the tomato slices in flour to coat on all sides. Then dip them into the egg mixture and finally press them into the breadcrumbs to coat all sides of the tomato.

5. Spray or brush the air-fryer oven with olive oil. Transfer 3 to 4 tomato slices into the air fryer oven and spray the top with olive oil. Air-fry the tomatoes at 400°F for 8 minutes. Flip them over, spray the other side with oil and air-fry for an additional 4 minutes until golden brown.

6. While the tomatoes are cooking, make the sriracha mayo. Combine the mayonnaise, 1 tablespoon of the sriracha hot sauce and milk in a small bowl. Stir well until the mixture is smooth. Add more sriracha sauce to taste.

7. When the tomatoes are done, transfer them to a cooling rack or a platter lined with paper towels so the bottom does not get soggy. Before serving, carefully stack the all the tomatoes into air fryer oven and air-fry at 350°F for 1 to 2 minutes to heat them back up.

8. Serve the fried green tomatoes hot with the sriracha mayo on the side. Season one last time with salt and freshly ground black pepper and garnish with sprigs of fresh thyme or chopped fresh chives.

DESSERTS

Cowboy Cookies

Servings: 3
Cooking Time: 14 Minutes

Ingredients:

- Recommended Hamilton Beach® Product: Stand Mixers
- 1 cup butter
- 1 cup sugar
- 1 cup light brown sugar
- 2 eggs
- 2 cups flour
- 1 teaspoon baking soda
- ½ teaspoon baking powder
- ½ teaspoon salt
- 2 cups oatmeal
- 1 tablespoon vanilla
- 12 ounces chocolate chips
- 1 ½ cups coconut

Directions:

1. Preheat the toaster oven to 350°F.
2. With flat beater attachment, cream together butter, sugar, and brown sugar at a medium setting until well blended. Mix in vanilla and eggs. Reduce speed and gradually add flour, baking soda, baking powder, and salt mix until smooth.
3. On a low setting, mix in oatmeal, chocolate chips, and coconut until well mixed. Drop rounded spoon full onto ungreased cookie sheet.
4. Bake on middle rack of oven for 12 to 14 minutes.

Chewy Brownies

Servings: 16

Cooking Time: 60 Minutes

Ingredients:

- 3 tablespoons Dutch-processed cocoa powder
- ¾ teaspoon espresso powder (optional)
- ⅓ cup boiling water
- 1 ounce unsweetened chocolate, chopped fine
- 5 tablespoons vegetable oil
- 2 tablespoons unsalted butter, melted and cooled
- 1¼ cups (8¾ ounces) sugar
- 1 large egg plus 1 large yolk
- 1 teaspoon vanilla extract
- ¾ cup (3¾ ounces) plus 2 tablespoons all-purpose flour
- 3 ounces bittersweet chocolate, cut into ½-inch pieces
- ½ teaspoon table salt

Directions:

1. Adjust toaster oven rack to middle position and preheat the toaster oven to 350 degrees. Make foil sling for 8-inch square baking pan by folding 2 long sheets of aluminum foil so each is 8 inches wide. Lay sheets of foil in pan perpendicular to each other, with extra foil hanging over edges of pan. Push foil into corners and up sides of pan, smoothing foil flush to pan. Spray foil with vegetable oil spray.

2. Whisk cocoa; espresso powder, if using; and boiling water together in large bowl until smooth. Add unsweetened chocolate and whisk until chocolate is melted. Whisk in oil and melted butter. (Mixture may look curdled.) Whisk in sugar, egg and yolk, and vanilla until smooth. Add flour, bittersweet chocolate, and salt and mix with rubber spatula until no dry flour remains.

3. Scrape batter into prepared pan, smooth top, and bake until toothpick inserted in center comes out with few moist crumbs attached, 25 to 30 minutes, rotating dish halfway through baking. Transfer pan to wire rack and cool for 1½ hours.

4. Using foil overhang, lift brownies from pan. Return brownies to wire rack and let cool completely, about 1 hour. Cut into 2-inch squares and serve.

Currant Carrot Cake

Servings: 6

Cooking Time: 30 Minutes

Ingredients:

- 1 cup unbleached flour
- 1 teaspoon baking powder
- 1 teaspoon baking soda
- ½ cup evaporated skim milk
- ½ cup brown sugar
- 2 tablespoons vegetable oil
- 1 egg
- 1 cup grated carrots
- ½ cup chopped currants
- ¼ cup finely chopped pecans
- Salt to taste
- Yogurt Cream Icing (recipe follows)

Directions:

1. Preheat the toaster oven to 350° F.
2. Combine all the ingredients in a medium bowl, stirring well to mix thoroughly.
3. Spread the batter in an oiled or nonstick 8½ × 8½ × 2-inch square baking (cake) pan.
4. BAKE for 30 minutes, or until a toothpick inserted in the center comes out clean. Cool on a wire rack. Ice with Yogurt Cream Icing.

Blueberry Clafoutis

Servings: 6

Cooking Time: 35 Minutes

Ingredients:

- 2 tablespoons salted butter, melted, plus extra for greasing the baking dish
- ½ cup all-purpose flour, plus extra for dusting the baking dish
- 2 cups fresh blueberries
- 1 cup whole milk
- 3 large eggs
- ½ cup granulated sugar
- ¼ cup light brown sugar
- 2 teaspoons vanilla extract

Directions:

1. Place the rack in position 1 and preheat the toaster oven to 350°F on BAKE for 5 minutes.
2. Lightly grease and flour a 9-inch-square baking dish.
3. Spread the blueberries in the bottom of the baking dish.
4. In a large bowl, whisk the milk, eggs, sugar, brown sugar, butter, and vanilla until smooth.
5. Add the flour and whisk to combine.
6. Pour the batter into the baking dish and bake for 35 minutes or until light brown and a toothpick inserted into the center comes out clean. If the top starts to get too brown, cover the dish lightly with foil.
7. Cool for 10 minutes and serve.

Giant Oatmeal–peanut Butter Cookie

Servings: 4

Cooking Time: 18 Minutes

Ingredients:

- 1 cup Rolled oats (not quick-cooking or steel-cut oats)
- ½ cup All-purpose flour
- ½ teaspoon Ground cinnamon
- ½ teaspoon Baking soda
- ⅓ cup Packed light brown sugar
- ¼ cup Solid vegetable shortening
- 2 tablespoons Natural-style creamy peanut butter
- 3 tablespoons Granulated white sugar
- 2 tablespoons (or 1 small egg, well beaten) Pasteurized egg substitute, such as Egg Beaters
- ⅓ cup Roasted, salted peanuts, chopped
- Baking spray

Directions:

1. Preheat the toaster oven to 350°F..
2. Stir the oats, flour, cinnamon, and baking soda in a bowl until well combined.
3. Using an electric hand mixer at medium speed, beat the brown sugar, shortening, peanut butter, granulated white sugar, and egg substitute or egg (as applicable) until smooth and creamy, about 3 minutes, scraping down the inside of the bowl occasionally.
4. Scrape down and remove the beaters. Fold in the flour mixture and peanuts with a rubber spatula just until all the flour is moistened and the peanut bits are evenly distributed in the dough.
5. For a small air fryer oven, coat the inside of a 6-inch round cake pan with baking spray. For a medium air fryer oven, coat the inside of a 7-inch round cake pan with baking spray. And for a large air fryer oven, coat the inside of an 8-inch round cake pan with baking spray. Scrape and gently press the dough into the prepared pan, spreading it into an even layer to the perimeter.
6. Set the pan in the air fryer oven and air-fry undisturbed for 18 minutes, or until well browned.
7. Transfer the pan to a wire rack and cool for 15 minutes. Loosen the cookie from the perimeter with a spatula, then invert the pan onto a cutting board and let the cookie come free. Remove the pan and reinvert the cookie onto the wire rack. Cool for 5 minutes more before slicing into wedges to serve.

Almond-roasted Pears

Servings: 4
Cooking Time: 15 Minutes

Ingredients:
- Yogurt Topping
- 1 container vanilla Greek yogurt (5–6 ounces)
- ¼ teaspoon almond flavoring
- 2 whole pears
- ¼ cup crushed Biscoff cookies (approx. 4 cookies)
- 1 tablespoon sliced almonds
- 1 tablespoon butter

Directions:
1. Stir almond flavoring into yogurt and set aside while preparing pears.
2. Halve each pear and spoon out the core.
3. Place pear halves in air fryer oven.
4. Stir together the cookie crumbs and almonds. Place a quarter of this mixture into the hollow of each pear half.
5. Cut butter into 4 pieces and place one piece on top of crumb mixture in each pear.
6. Preheat the toaster oven to 400°F and air-fry for 15 minutes or until pears have cooked through but are still slightly firm.
7. Serve pears warm with a dollop of yogurt topping.

Orange Glaze

Servings: 1
Cooking Time: 10 Minutes

Ingredients:
- 1 cup orange juice
- ½ cup sugar

Directions:
1. Combine the orange juice and sugar in a small bowl and mix well. Transfer the mixture to a baking pan.
2. BROIL for 10 minutes, stirring after 5 minutes, or until the sugar is dissolved and the liquid is reduced. Drizzle on top of brownies and cool. Cut into squares and serve with scoops of vanilla frozen yogurt or orange sherbet.

Lime Cheesecake

Servings: 6
Cooking Time: 30 Minutes

Ingredients:
- Oil spray (hand-pumped)
- ½ cup graham cracker crumbs
- 24 ounces cream cheese, room temperature
- 1½ cups granulated sugar
- 4 large eggs
- ¼ cup sour cream
- Juice and zest of 1 lime
- 2 teaspoons vanilla extract

Directions:
1. Place the rack in position 1 and preheat the oven to 350°F on BAKE for 5 minutes.
2. Lightly spray an 8-inch springform pan with the oil and spread the graham cracker crumbs in the bottom.
3. Bake for 10 minutes, then remove the crust from the air fryer and set it aside.
4. In a large bowl, beat the cream cheese until very smooth with an electric hand beater. Add the sugar by ½-cup measures, beating very well after each addition and scraping down the sides of the bowl.
5. Add the eggs one at a time, beating well after each addition and scraping down the sides of the bowl.
6. Beat in the sour cream, lime juice, lime zest, and vanilla until very well blended and fluffy, about 4 minutes.
7. Transfer the batter to the pan and smooth the top.
8. Bake for 30 minutes or until set.
9. Let the cheesecake cool in the oven for 30 minutes and then transfer to the refrigerator to cool completely. Serve.

Easy Peach Turnovers

Servings: 6

Cooking Time: 35 Minutes

Ingredients:

- 1 ½ tablespoons granulated sugar
- 1 teaspoon cornstarch
- ¾ cup chopped peeled peaches, fresh or frozen and thawed
- ½ teaspoon grated lemon zest
- ⅛ teaspoon ground nutmeg
- Dash table salt
- 1 sheet frozen puff pastry, about 9 inches square, thawed (½ of a 17.3-ounce package)
- 1 large egg
- Coarse white sugar
- GLAZE
- ¾ cup confectioners' sugar
- ½ teaspoon pure vanilla extract
- 1 to 2 tablespoons milk

Directions:

1. Line a 12 x 12-inch baking pan with parchment paper.

2. Stir the granulated sugar and cornstarch in a medium bowl. Stir in the peaches, lemon zest, nutmeg, and salt. Mix until the sugar-cornstarch mixture coats the peaches evenly and the sugar begins to dissolve; set aside.

3. On a lightly floured board, roll the puff pastry sheet into a 13 ½ x 9-inch rectangle. Cut the puff pastry into 6 (4 ½-inch) squares. Lightly beat the egg in a small bowl, then brush the edges of each puff pastry square with the egg. Reserve the remaining egg to brush on top of each turnover.

4. Spoon about 2 tablespoons peach mixture into the center of each square. Fold the pastry over the peaches to form a triangle, pinching to seal the edges. Using the tines of a fork, crimp the edges tightly. Lightly brush the top of each turnover with the egg. Sprinkle each with the coarse sugar.

5. Place the turnovers on the prepared pan. Freeze the turnovers for 15 minutes.

6. Preheat the toaster oven to 375°F. Bake for 15 to 20 minutes or until golden brown. Let cool 5 to 10 minutes.

7. Meanwhile make the glaze: Whisk the confectioners' sugar, vanilla, and 1 tablespoon milk in a small bowl until smooth. If needed, stir in the additional milk to reach the desired consistency. Drizzle the glaze from the tip of a teaspoon in decorative stripes over the turnovers.

Keto Cheesecake Cups

Servings: 6
Cooking Time: 10 Minutes

Ingredients:
- 8 ounces cream cheese
- ¼ cup plain whole-milk Greek yogurt
- 1 large egg
- 1 teaspoon pure vanilla extract
- 3 tablespoons monk fruit sweetener
- ¼ teaspoon salt
- ½ cup walnuts, roughly chopped

Directions:
1. Preheat the toaster oven to 315°F.
2. In a large bowl, use a hand mixer to beat the cream cheese together with the yogurt, egg, vanilla, sweetener, and salt. When combined, fold in the chopped walnuts.
3. Set 6 silicone muffin liners inside an air-fryer-safe pan.
4. Evenly fill the cupcake liners with cheesecake batter.
5. Carefully place the pan into the air fryer oven and air-fry for about 10 minutes, or until the tops are lightly browned and firm.
6. Carefully remove the pan when done and place in the refrigerator for 3 hours to firm up before serving.

Hasselback Apple Crisp

Servings: 4

Cooking Time: 20 Minutes

Ingredients:

- 2 large Gala apples, peeled, cored and cut in half
- ¼ cup butter, melted
- ½ teaspoon ground cinnamon
- 2 tablespoons sugar
- Topping
- 3 tablespoons butter, melted
- 2 tablespoons brown sugar
- ¼ cup chopped pecans
- 2 tablespoons rolled oats
- 1 tablespoon flour
- vanilla ice cream
- caramel sauce

Directions:

1. Place the apples cut side down on a cutting board. Slicing from stem end to blossom end, make 8 to 10 slits down the apple halves but only slice three quarters of the way through the apple, not all the way through to the cutting board.

2. Preheat the toaster oven to 330°F and pour a little water into the bottom of the air fryer oven drawer. (This will help prevent the grease that drips into the bottom drawer from burning and smoking.)

3. Transfer the apples to the air fryer oven, flat side down. Combine ¼ cup of melted butter, cinnamon and sugar in a small bowl. Brush this butter mixture onto the apples and air-fry at 330°F for 15 minutes. Baste the apples several times with the butter mixture during the cooking process.

4. While the apples are air-frying, make the filling. Combine 3 tablespoons of melted butter with the brown sugar, pecans, rolled oats and flour in a bowl. Stir with a fork until the mixture resembles small crumbles.

5. When the timer on the air fryer oven is up, spoon the topping down the center of the apples. Air-fry at 330°F for an additional 5 minutes.

6. Transfer the apples to a serving plate and serve with vanilla ice cream and caramel sauce.

Individual Peach Crisps

Servings: 2
Cooking Time: 60 Minutes

Ingredients:

- 2 tablespoons granulated sugar, divided
- 1 teaspoon lemon juice
- ¼ teaspoon cornstarch
- ⅛ teaspoon table salt, divided
- 1 pound frozen sliced peaches, thawed
- ⅓ cup whole almonds or pecans, chopped fine
- ¼ cup (1¼ ounces) all-purpose flour
- 2 tablespoons packed light brown sugar
- ⅛ teaspoon ground cinnamon
- Pinch ground nutmeg
- 3 tablespoons unsalted butter, melted and cooled

Directions:

1. Adjust toaster oven rack to lowest position and preheat the toaster oven to 425 degrees. Combine 1 tablespoon granulated sugar, lemon juice, cornstarch, and pinch salt in medium bowl. Gently toss peaches with sugar mixture and divide evenly between two 12-ounce ramekins.

2. Combine almonds, flour, brown sugar, cinnamon, nutmeg, remaining pinch salt, and remaining 1 tablespoon granulated sugar in now-empty bowl. Drizzle with melted butter and toss with fork until evenly moistened and mixture forms large chunks with some pea-size pieces throughout. Sprinkle topping evenly over peaches, breaking up any large chunks.

3. Place ramekins on aluminum foil–lined small rimmed baking sheet and bake until filling is bubbling around edges and topping is deep golden brown, 25 to 30 minutes, rotating sheet halfway through baking. Let crisps cool on wire rack for 15 minutes before serving.

Green Grape Meringues

Servings: 4
Cooking Time: 40 Minutes

Ingredients:

- 1 cup sugar
- 3 egg whites, beaten until stiff
- ½ teaspoon lemon juice
- Vanilla frozen yogurt
- 1 cup sliced fresh green grapes
- 2 squares unsweetened baking chocolate, shaved
- Nonfat whipped topping

Directions:

1. Preheat the toaster oven to 250° F.

2. Add the sugar slowly to the egg white mixture and continue to beat. Add the lemon juice. With a tablespoon, drop on an oiled or nonstick 6½ × 10-inch baking sheet to make a mound of meringue approximately 2 inches across. Make a slight depression in the center of each one.

3. BAKE for 40 minutes, or until crusty and browned. Cool and fill each meringue shell with a scoop of vanilla frozen yogurt. Top with equal portions of green grapes, chocolate shavings, and nonfat whipped topping. The meringues may be stored in an airtight container until ready to use.

Spice Cake

Servings: 6

Cooking Time: 25 Minutes

Ingredients:

- 1 cup applesauce or 2 4-ounce jars baby food prunes
- ¼ cup skim milk or low-fat soy milk
- 1 tablespoon vegetable oil
- ½ cup brown sugar
- 1 egg
- 1½ cups unbleached flour
- 1 teaspoon baking powder
- ½ teaspoon baking soda
- ¼ teaspoon grated nutmeg
- ½ teaspoon ground cinnamon
- ½ teaspoon grated orange zest
- Salt to taste
- Creamy Frosting

Directions:

1. Preheat the toaster oven to 350° F.
2. Stir together the applesauce, milk, oil, sugar, and egg in a small bowl. Set aside.
3. Combine the flour, baking powder, nutmeg, cinnamon, orange zest, and salt in a medium bowl. Add the applesauce mixture and stir to mix well. Pour the batter into an oiled or nonstick 8½ × 8½ × 2-inch square baking (cake) pan.
4. BAKE for 25 minutes, or until a toothpick inserted in the center comes out clean. Frost with Creamy Frosting.

Gingerbread

Servings: 6
Cooking Time: 20 Minutes

Ingredients:

- cooking spray
- 1 cup flour
- 2 tablespoons sugar
- ¾ teaspoon ground ginger
- ¼ teaspoon cinnamon
- 1 teaspoon baking powder
- ½ teaspoon baking soda
- ⅛ teaspoon salt
- 1 egg
- ¼ cup molasses
- ½ cup buttermilk
- 2 tablespoons oil
- 1 teaspoon pure vanilla extract

Directions:

1. Preheat the toaster oven to 330°F.
2. Spray 6 x 6-inch baking dish lightly with cooking spray.
3. In a medium bowl, mix together all the dry ingredients.
4. In a separate bowl, beat the egg. Add molasses, buttermilk, oil, and vanilla and stir until well mixed.
5. Pour liquid mixture into dry ingredients and stir until well blended.
6. Pour batter into baking dish and Air-fry at 330°F for 20 minutes or until toothpick inserted in center of loaf comes out clean.

Pineapple Tartlets

Servings: 4

Cooking Time: 20 Minutes

Ingredients:

- Vegetable oil
- 6 sheets phyllo pastry
- 1 8-ounce can crushed pineapple, drained
- 3 tablespoons low-fat cottage cheese
- 2 tablespoons orange or pineapple marmalade
- 6 teaspoons concentrated thawed frozen orange juice
- Vanilla frozen yogurt or nonfat whipped topping

Directions:

1. Preheat the toaster oven to 350° F.

2. Brush the pans of a 6-muffin tin with vegetable oil. Lay a phyllo sheet on a clean, flat surface and brush with oil. Fold the sheet into quarters to fit the muffin pan. Repeat the process for the remaining phyllo sheets and pans.

3. BAKE for 5 minutes, or until lightly browned. Remove from the oven and cool.

4. Combine the pineapple, cottage cheese, and marmalade in a small bowl, mixing well. Fill the phyllo shells (in the pans) with equal portions of the mixture. Drizzle 1 teaspoon orange juice concentrate over each.

5. BAKE at 400° F. for 15 minutes, or until the filling is cooked. Cool and remove the tartlets carefully from the muffin pans to dessert dishes. Top with vanilla frozen yogurt or nonfat whipped topping.

Blueberry Cookies

Servings: 4

Cooking Time: 12 Minutes

Ingredients:

- 1 egg
- 1 tablespoon margarine, at room temperature
- ⅓ cup sugar
- 1¼ cups unbleached flour
- Salt to taste
- 1 teaspoon baking powder
- 1 10-ounce package frozen blueberries, well drained, or
- 1½ cups fresh blueberries, rinsed and drained

Directions:

1. Preheat the toaster oven to 400° F.

2. Beat together the egg, margarine, and sugar in a medium bowl with an electric mixer until smooth. Add the flour, salt, and baking powder, mixing thoroughly. Gently stir in the blueberries just to blend. Do not overmix.

3. Drop by teaspoonfuls on an oiled or nonstick 6½ × 10-inch baking sheet or an oiled or nonstick 8½ × 8½ × 2-inch square baking (cake) pan.

4. BAKE for 12 minutes, or until the cookies are golden brown.

Printed by Libri Plureos GmbH in Hamburg,
Germany